Madder

This work is for
my mother   [my father]
who gave me
this.

This is not how it happened at all.

What is the truest fact of your life?

You've got it all wrong.

La madrugada estalla como una estatua
Como una estatua de alas que se dispersan por la ciudad
Y el mediodía canta campana de agua
Campana de agua de oro que nos prohíbe la soledad
Y la noche levanta su copa larga
su larga copa larga, luna temprana por sobre el mar
Pero para María no hay madrugada,
pero para María no hay mediodía,
pero para María ninguna luna,
alza su copa roja sobre las aguas . . .
María no tiene tiempo (María Landó)
de alzar los ojos
María de alzar los ojos (María Landó)
rotos de sueño
María rotos de sueño (María Landó)
de andar sufriendo
María de andar sufriendo (María Landó)
sólo trabaja
María sólo trabaja, sólo trabaja, sólo trabaja
María sólo trabaja
y su trabajo es ajeno
María Landó, María Landó, María Landó,
María Landó sólo trabaja,
María Landó sólo trabaja,
María Landó sólo trabaja
María Landó sólo trabaja
y su trabajo es ajeno

—*César Calvo, "María Landó," as sung by Susana Baca*

[
Someone hides from someone else
Hides under his tongue
The other looks for him under the earth

He hides on his forehead
The other looks for him in the sky

He hides inside his forgetfulness
The other looks for him in the grass

Looks for him looks
There's no place he doesn't look
And looking he loses himself

—Vasko Popa, "Hide-and-Seek"

]

Contents

Madder

Ground

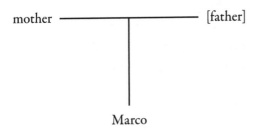

mother ———————— [father]

Marco

Weeds, This Semblance

I am a gardener, this birthright from grandmother and mother and aunt passed down and diagonally to me. A stolen bit of history, inútil, this useless love. For much of my adult life I have worked my hands through plant leaves and plant roots; worked my mind through folklore and Latin names, soil and air; worked myself into this semblance of a garden, staving off the weeds.

But the more I garden the less I weed. Burdock's root reaches too deep. Madder runs riot through the back places. Shepherd's purse gives itself away to the wind heart- by heart- by heart-shaped seed. Instead I forage. I make friends with the excessive and out-of-place, this unkempt garden. My life, these weeds.

A weed is excessive, too good for its own or anyone else's good. Virtuosic in its reach and fecundity. It exceeds expectations. An overachiever, it surprises and perplexes when so little was asked of it.

A weed is out of place. It cannot say how it got here, to this lonely spot. To say it has pilgrimed here would suppose intention and a singular trip carried out in one body to one place. Rather this travel has been going on endlessly across generations: a nomadic life. One day, out of places: here.

I am a gardener and find myself year after year less able to do what is necessary to keep up the semblance of a garden. Redbud seedlings invade and I think of the rough nodules of their roots fixing nitrogen in the soil. Spiderwort fountains out of unexpected places, but its flowers are the purple-blue of the deepest summer-twilight sky. Dandelions are not even weeds to me anymore, to my neighbor's great disappointment, but bitter tonic in salads, rich sweetness in tea, acidy pickles in pasta, cheerful reminder to be optimistic even in desperate circumstances.

As I write this, my seventy-three-year-old mother, who has been visiting us for a month due to waning health, is outside vigorously, single-mindedly, furiously hacking at weeds coming up between the flagstones of our front walk. For her there is no question of order and its need, of the immorality of weeds or their excision. Some things must not be allowed to rise up. Though she is resolute, I can't tell anymore if my life is choked with weeds or nothing but them. Whether to make a reckoning of it means clearing a little space of legibility or taking field notes on the little and the many that populate this space, this semblance, this life. I cannot tell, except by telling.

I forage this little life from here and there. Violet leaves from the lawn, sumac seeds from the highway shoulder, wild grapes off the chain-link fence. I dry summer's linden flowers for the winter. I dig up and casket shovel-killer dock roots in alcohol, reinterred in my basement as medicine for the future. I ferment cloves of garlic in honey, preserving one and transforming both.

I do all these things because I want to remember. Remember that the little and the useless are what knit the visible world together. Remember that there is no such thing as absence, only ache.

I do this haphazardly, without efficiency or logic. Scrape the root to the bright core to stain this blank page. Scry meaning from the resulting patterns, worrying the contours between memory and fantasy and oblivion. Assemble bones into a body I've never seen before. Lay seeds where its heart might be.

I am a gardener who can no longer garden, so painfully in love am I with everything that might be. These thousands of gardens of the mind all live, overlaying each other in possibility. How to undo one for another? How to pluck out for the withering heap one life and not mourn? So much, dissembled, has confused the maps. So much is taken away from us, and so early.

This morning I sent a card to my eighty-seven-year-old father (seventeen years after the last one), directed to an address whose front door has never opened for me. I can peer down from space at the light-brown roof, the white concrete driveway, and a red sedan thanks to Google Maps, but I can't fly down into the branches of the tree out front and search wordlessly through a window. There is an artificial pond behind the house, the heart of this little ring of suburban houses. A diffuse white explosion in the center must be an aerator spraying water into the air, but I can't soar through prismatic space and get caught on a breeze to land and evaporate in an instant on the back of his papery, wrinkled, spotted hand, resting on the arm of his favorite back-patio armchair. Street View cameras mounted atop a car haven't crawled along his street yet, so I can't stare at his front door and wonder what knocking on it might be like.

I can't tell you what I wrote because I didn't have the forethought to transcribe it, and my daily missives to him vanish in my mind so quickly, like rain that falls over the desert and evaporates before hitting the ground. I cannot tell you if he received it, if desert rain even knows its fated trajectory or what ground even is. Dead ground, living ground: who can tell me what grows there, where rain never reaches?

Between a pathway razed meticulously and the void of the desert: a small patch of weeds, a garden, a semblance of a garden, a life.

A weed is of no use to one who has no use for it. If you let me, I will thatch my roof in phragmites, wattle my walls with buckthorn, plumb this hut with hollow knotweed stems, and pipe tunes through this ramshackle body until it shakes with fever or dance. I will burn up this uselessness—what my family used to call me my whole childhood, *inútil*. I will burn up this uselessness to keep warm. I will burn up this uselessness to tell a story by, until the world around me catches fire. I will burn up this uselessness until this uselessness has had done with the useful.

Matter

"La madrugada estalla . . ."

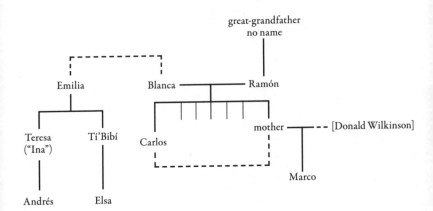

Root: Burdock

Arctium lappa, L

Burdock, possibly *beurre*-dock, relic of migration, footprint on
the shore.

Little bear, rough burr, this is your sweet beurre offering:
she carried you across the autumn fields of time, small snag of flesh,
into dream and out of it into world.

1: Beggar's Buttons

*
* *

I remember:

*
* *

My aunt Tí'Bibí* grew rows of corn and towers of tomatoes in ordered abundance in her backyard. The backyard I only remember as green and gold and blue light. The backyard where pure water from the hose geysered a plastic hat from a children's water game high into the air and I jumped through the jet, shrieking in glee as the hat came down.

The backyard . . . I was only three or four years old . . . that dropped off past the chain-link fence down a precipitous cliff of fine sand molded by rains into colorless lava flows, so much shifting fill. And in the distance the half-constructed houses. The concrete foundations like swimming pools. The wild and uncharted terraforming of what was probably once pine woods into yet another sleepy weave of curving streets. House after house for perfect families that I was already beginning to understand would never be mine.

And there in the sandy scrub of the soft descent to this new world in the making were my older cousins Elsa and Andrés clambering down the slope to play in the houses of the future— always ahead three or four footfalls of soft sand giving way in little avalanches, always running away. And there, the dried-out hooks, the seedheads of burdock catching on my little shirt as I slid in anxious pursuit lest they leave me behind.

---

* I call her my aunt, and *Tí* is short for *tía,* but really she was my mother's cousin (and even that is stretching the definition, but that's a story for later). Bibí isn't really her name, just the nickname that everyone uses for her rather than her true name, Elsa, which I don't think I ever heard anyone call her. The extended family I grew up in was a maze of nicknames always steering away from true names and histories.

Little burr, small reminder of my own attempts to catch a ride, to stow along, to a family with a father and a mother and a purchase on some portion of stability. You too are calling out, "Bear me"; searching, searching, tearing at the stitches of others' lives, trying to make your way into the weave.

*
* *

Burdock is a rough plant, growing in the tumble of hedgerows and forest edges, against the edge of a stone path where it cannot be dislodged. It is persistent, impertinent. Its rough, warty leaves fountain blue and green from petioles, bloody as bruises. Its stalk, tenacious and stringy, with streaks of violet, terminates in tender pink pricks of little thistle flowers that, drying, unfurl their claws. Its taproot runs deep and thick into the clenching earth.

*
* *

Arctium, from *arktos,* "bear"; *lappa,* "to seize"

Bear burr, rough
wild growl in the hedge
at the edge
of the field
patrolling the perimeter.
Little bear burrowing
in your den, deep excavations
uncover sweetness but you're
not going anywhere without a fight.

Paw at me, rough me up.
Scratched cheeks run through
the field and the autumn sun
fills the emptied-out blue sky.
Your sleuth of siblings all
menace with spikes, barbs, fangs, and claws,
but you little bear bury
your tiny nails in
and hug, hang, hanker for
some new home away from here
before the winter crashes in.
Mother's soft underbelly,
moist leaves and duff,
rub your cheek
into the ground
and pray
you make it
until spring.

*
* *

Across the north, the Bear lays her starry lap against the sky and
tilts a nose toward her cub. The Greeks looked north, and in the
mountains among the barbarians she patrolled in the night,
the arktos. Rough fur wrapped against the snowy winds in the
passes. A guttural string of confusion for speech. Language from
another land, out of place.

*
* *

My mother would leave the textile factory at eleven p.m. and head to Bibí's, her little red Volkswagen with the white pleather interior weaving up the curving slope with its headlights illuminating the frosty fog, until it pulled up to the little cape house and the engine's purr stuttered into an idle and then swallowed itself into the cold silence. She was there to retrieve her toddler son from the care of her cousin, as she did every night. Later, it would be Bibí's sister, Teresa, who would take care of me while my mother worked, but in those first moments of consciousness bubbling up into the possibility of memory, it was my Tí'Bibí's face quietly smiling as she eased me into a crib at night. Did my own mother ever quite forgive her for that?

*
* *

("You've got it all wrong.
This is not how it happened at all,"
my mother says.)

*
* *

As Tí'Bibí and Tío Julio slept in the room across the hall, my mother stole the soft, pliable form out of the crib and wrapped him in an icy-blue boiled-wool blanket wreathed in dark-blue flowers, its pilled-up surface rough but warm.

The stairs creaked as she descended to the front door, the screen door's chain tinkled, and the aluminum latch clicked as it fell softly, deliberately into place, though the car door's close always sounded too loudly like a shout into the cold, thin night air, and then the rumble of the car engine returned to a purr winding back down the street.

Back at her own apartment, she climbed the stairs, hooking the blue parcel tight in her arms. It squirmed, woke, moved closer.

*
* *

Arctium lappa is a common weed. Native to Eurasia, but naturalized across the globe. Cosmopolitan alien. Industrious immigrant.

Elsa, Andrés, and I were the children of another land, seed fallen in another field. As is common in so many immigrant families, we code-switched, answering our parents' native language with that of our own native tongue. Which is to say that we all spoke Rhode Island English to our parents' Ríoplatense Spanish and laid down linguistic borders and checkpoints, securing our little lives against the terror of being other.

In grade school did you also have a deep, pressing anxiety that you were not learning English the right way? That you could not handle the idioms of your world or wield a joke adequately?

Did we all secretly hate our parents for opening their mouths?

*
* *

My great-grandfather was apparently a stowaway from the coast of Africa to the shores of South America. When he hid in the hold of the ship, did he have help, a conspirator, a coyote? Did he pay his way at some hidden ticket counter, or was the voyage on credit paid out over years in sweat on the other side? Looking at the dragon trees of the Islas Canarias, did he imagine the Ombú of Uruguay? In the belly of this wooden whale plunged into the water, did leaves turn to roots, his roots into legs? Did he change his name, baptized in the muddy Río de la Plata? Did he walk off the ship or was he thrown?

No one in my family now knows or cares what he did or why, though he was my grandfather's father, not so far removed.

*
* *

Burdock, like dandelion and so many other tap-rooted plants, is tenacious and resists removal. Deliberately brittle, the main root, though it is removed, will always break and leave some tail of a rootlet behind. Like a lizard in reverse, each tail regrows its own body, new yet identical to all the others.

*
* *

People from Canelones in Uruguay, where my family took root, are all "Canarios" regardless of origin.

*
* *

Brittle root, resist removal
but if you must, then leave
some of yourself behind.

Lateral roots remain wrenched
in clenching gray clay.
Where there was one

now three will be.
Birdsong in the breeze,
spice from horseradish
leaves carried in a stiff wind.
When harvesting, separate
the sons from the potent father
root and plant them back in the family plot.

*
* *

Who did great-grandfather no-name leave behind? Did the village in the mountains wave him down the stony road with white handkerchiefs and whistles? Or did he pepper the hills with sons and a hunting party whistle him into the bowels of a boat? Remove the father, root the sons.

[My mother wanted a son of her own at any cost. Remove the father, root the son.]

*
* *

By root or by bee, deep underground or caught up on the run, how did I come to be? How many times can you break the brittle root before it is exhausted?

2: A Well, A Ladder

*
* *

My mother's family used to live in the back country, among thick earthen walls stitched with hay and under thatch expertly laid by the quinchero making his never-ending circular pilgrimage across the land. In the dark, smoky kitchen there was the endless kneading of dough—that mix of punch and caress, punch and caress, meting out the days unseen. In the dark, drafty barn, little more than a lean-to, there was the milking of the cow and the leers and crude jokes of her brothers. In the dark, rank chicken coop there was the foraging for shit-stained eggs under the pecking glare of the chickens and the restrained, lip-bitten wish for something more than this flightless, imprisoned life of wasted work. (Oh to produce more than just someone else's full belly. Oh to produce a son for herself.)

My mother has two birthdays, March 14 and March 18. The first, her entry into the world from between her mother Blanca's legs. The second, her entry into the town ledger four days later, when her father, Ramón, managed to finalize her birth into existence. Was the wait really, as is always told, because the country was so formidable, the road so long, the work of the land so pressing? Of what use this squirming mass? Candle her by the lantern and she comes up empty of seed, only a daily procession of toil, each day of kneading and milking and scrubbing curled like a tiny egg inside her.

What good is the burr empty of seed? At least it has the possibility of escape, but in the end what does it produce?

*
* *

"Pinochet! Pinochet!" I called out, smiling as my grandfather Ramón's sweet little dog came running on clicking black nails across the cracked concrete floor of the patio, his blond tail wagging furiously. I was ten years old and visiting Uruguay with my mother for the second time in my life (the first was when I was four). In the afternoons I sat with my grandfather outside at a rickety wooden table and learned to play the card game conga, or he would try unsuccessfully to teach me a game that involved tossing goat knuckles on the ground. His stubbled wattle flapped cheerfully on the narrowest of necks, and his wild eyebrows fluttered as he cackled, "Un día serás el presidente de América!" (One day you'll be president of America!) Then he would gum with satisfaction the softly disintegrating stub of the hand-rolled cigarette that he had been nursing for hours.

I understood instinctively maybe half of what all the strange people around me were saying but was wholly incapable of responding. I clung close to my mother, who served as translator. Occasionally it became clear that more was being said than was being translated, or more was not being said at all in any language but was being communicated with silence, pursed lips, and penetrating stares. On that trip I had been reading a science-fiction novel whose plot involved Nazis, and on the cover was a swastika. One day I was warned by my older cousins that under no circumstances should I leave this book out for my grandfather to see. Their startled eyes and dark expressions, coupled with quick words completely lost on me, meant the book stayed out of sight, though I imagine had he seen it, my grandfather, who never heard of a dictator he didn't admire, would have cackled with glee and patted me on the back for knowing a great man when I saw one.

*
* *

It hardly mattered that the principal of the one-room schoolhouse came to my grandparents' door to beg them not to pull their eleven-year-old daughter from school because she was so promising. To make ends meet, there were the endless napkins to wash and iron for the local restaurant, so her small hands lifted the wooden-handled iron's lid to drop in the coals and snapped it back shut. She walked outside to swing it like a censer, shaking off plumes of white ash lest they smudge the pristine white cloth, and went back inside to resume the ironing and the folding for hours on end. But let it not be said that my mother's parents had no ears to hear the principal's pleas—they graciously let my mother finish the sixth grade, more than she needed, but that was enough. (Decades later, when Blanca passes away, how devastated my mother will be when she finds out over a crackling phone line half a world away that her little iron, emblem of her martyrdom, was given away to a distant relative with hardly a thought.)

*
* *

The rain poured mercilessly off the roof tiles of the farmhouse. Standing under the corrugated tin roof of the adjoining shed felt like being inside her head, which was explosively thrumming with the white noise of terror that was her feeling for her mother.

My mother, twelve years old, stood at the edge of the drip line of her aunt's house, feeling stray drops of the deluge sting her cold as she watched the summer thunderstorm span the dark horizon of the fields. It would not be so bad, she had convinced herself, to walk the mile along the dirt road out from the farm to the paved road lined with massive eucalyptus, where she could wait for the bus to come and take her back home to where her mother, Blanca, expected her. The lightning would surprise and the thunder would tremble her guts like jelly, but what of it? The bus might take its time or break down before reaching her, and she would have to stand under a flap of eucalyptus bark peeling off a trunk for a useless bit of shelter, but she'd had worse.

"No, no. ¿Cómo que vas a salir en esta tormenta? Te quedás aquí. Punto." (No, no. What do you mean you're going to go out in this storm? You'll stay here and that's all there is to it.) Her aunt Emilia would not consider any other option. Blanca would understand that, with the weather, her daughter had stayed at the farm. There were no phones, but a phone wasn't necessary. Care for the well-being of daughters and nieces was enough.

She sobbed, the white thrum of the rain pelting the tin roof finally spilling out of her head in hot tears and from her tremoring lips in strings of spit. No matter how hard she tried to contain it, the storm inside her exploded. It was afternoon and Emilia and her six daughters were sitting in a circle drinking maté. They passed the maté and sipped from the metal bombilla, watching the rain and the whipping branches of the trees, gasping and giggling at their gasping each time the lightning struck and thunder rolled through their bodies.

My mother didn't join them, just stood there sobbing in anticipation of the slap of the belt and the bellowing yells of her mother when she finally did return home. How many times had she yearned on these visits to stay with the chuckling circle of girls and their mother? How many times did she also secretly cultivate a twisted hatred for them and their easy ways?

She was right to sob, and to yearn, and to hate. When she eventually got home, she got all the beating, and more, that she had feared.

*
* *

("You've got it all wrong.
This is not how it happened at all,"
my grandparents say.)

*
* *

Was the beating for disobedience or for the lack of courage to face the lightning and pelting rain and shattering eucalyptus limbs falling in the road; for the five hundred napkins waiting to be ironed; or for the brothers who needed to be fed, cleaned up after, and humored?

Or was it for the suspicion that she preferred life in that other house, that house of all sisters and a kind mother—that she delayed on purpose?

Back to her cage! Back to her iron! And don't forget to swing the ashes away to keep the cloth white!

*
* *

Between memory and fantasy, oblivion.

*
* *

Soca: my mother's hometown.

Visiting now, all that can be said is "Poor Soca." Poor dusty plaza almost always completely empty. Poor high curbs by the two derelict bars, steps built into them that no one climbs anymore. Little weed in the fields, persisting in the hot sun, little noticed, off-track, holding on.

But when my mother was a child, before the Ruta Interbalnearia had been built along the coast through the beach towns, it was through Soca that all the excursions of Sunday beachgoers would pass, out of sweltering Montevideo on their way to the healthful restorative ocean breezes of places like La Floresta, Atlántida, and Costa Azul. One pass through in the morning and a stop for some freshly baked bizcochos, vigilantes of flaky dough covered in sugar, or cañones, little cones of the same flaky dough filled with either dulce de leche or cream. Or maybe just a simple toast with thin, glistening slices of ruby-red dulce de membrillo. And maybe a small porcelain cup of coffee to make up for the early start and hurried departure from the apartment in Pocitos or Prado or Punta Carretas to catch the tour bus before it backed out of its slanted bay in the corner of the Plaza de Independencia downtown. And for each of this urban crowd, dressed in their Sunday best, a pure-white cloth napkin awaited, pressed and creased with tears and resentment, flung away unnoticed as each napkin floated and settled in its destined lap, and then onto a plate, a seat, or the floor.

Then, with a neatly tied packet of resfuerzos, ham and cheese sandwiches on chilled white buttered bread with crusts cut off, the crowd was off, down the eucalyptus-shaded road to La

Floresta, where the beach and the ocean and their carefree Sunday awaited them.

*
* *

I am not telling the truth. I am letting you in on what I have stolen from the sealed archives, overheard from around corners, wrenched from clenched hands by screaming and shouting, fantasized out of thin air into a cobweb of a life.

*
* *

Between memory and oblivion, fantasy.

*
* *

Almost before the dust of the road settled in the buses' wake, preparations for their return were being made. Tables were cleared, floors were swept and mopped, dishes and silverware clattered into the restaurants' steaming sinks and out in women's reddened hands, bottles of whiskey were carted into the bars from storage sheds, a new mountain of crisp napkins was brought up from behind the counters. In the plaza, green with freshly watered lawns and vibrant with beds of annuals, ladders sprouted with men stringing lights from palm to palm.

My mother never saw any of this, not the morning arrivals nor the pouring of the coffees nor the flurry of white unfolded without a thought onto laps and equally unconsciously dropped in a tousled pile on a plate of crumbs, nor the afternoon rest and the stringing of the lights in the plaza.

*
*   *

All of this is a fantasy, but doesn't the imagination have its own life too? My mother has a few times in my life reminisced about how Soca used to be a busy crossroads and in only the direst moments confessed her rage at the curse of the coal-stoked little iron, but everything in between can only be surmised.

I once suggested she might want to speak with a counselor or therapist to work though painful memories. "Why would I do that? No one wants to hear what I have to say." And so (almost) nothing has ever been said.

*
*   *

Saturdays were for stoking coals to white heat, dropping them in the white enamel-handled iron's belly, swinging the iron just outside the door in the bright light trying to steer clear of the swirling ash, and then plunging into the gloom of the kitchen to press her fury into each white square, watching the orange glow of the embers through slits in the iron like a demon's eyes instructing her in the ways of hate. Saturday was for the town.

Sunday was for the farm: rake out the mucked hay from the chicken coop. Weed the potatoes, tend to the growing tobacco plants, make the run with kitchen slop to the pig's pen and tip it in quickly before the sow tackled her in its frenzy. Run the brothers' clothes across the ribbed zinc washboard until her knuckles were skinned, bring her father his pouch of tobacco and rolling papers, his maté, and a thermos of hot water (if he happened to be home that weekend from the work camp in the countryside where he cut down eucalyptus to be pressed for oil, a place he seemed to prefer to his own home). Do all of this with the sound of the buses rumbling into town on the main road in the distance.

If, and only if, she finished all these tasks in time—and if her cousins from La Floresta came, which helped immeasurably— she might be allowed to walk into town for the evening's festivities. As the summer day finally wound down into twilight, the buses returned with their passengers both energized and tired by their beachside frolics. Now the bulbs hanging over the paths in the plaza woke up, their naked filaments burning bright like hovering fireflies, and the time for flirting and courting and mischief began with the first opening lines of a tango or a milonga pouring out of the gramophone set up on a table in the center of the plaza (or more rarely from musicians playing live). In the plaza, swooping melodies of bandoneón and violin. In the bars, the tinkling of ice in whiskey against glass. Away from the lights, laughter.

*
* *

("You've got it all wrong.
This is not how any of this happened,"
all the ghosts say.)

*
* *

Little iron: swing through the air, cast off ashes, embers burning bright.

I want to see my mother in the couples dancing, or at a table in the bar nearly crying with laughter. Is her long copper hair swinging freely down her back or is it put up? Does she wear a dress she keeps put away for only these dances? Are there high heels?

*
* *

How could I tell you the truth when I don't know it myself? Instead I will curse you with this life in your hands. If you can break the curse, please come and tell me how.

*
* *

When she was old enough to finally refuse the iron, my mother hitched a ride to the capital and found freedom from slavery in servitude. In a well, any ladder will do.

A young woman, she climbed first the steps of the bus that took her to Montevideo, and then the floors of an apartment building in the elevator whose polished brass accordion-shutter gate tinkled elegantly at each story. For the Jewish family at the end of this ascension she cleaned floors, cared for children, carefully ironed tablecloths and napkins, learned to cook strange foods—and it was like heaven.

*
* *

Scratched off a haunch, nimbly plucked off a hem or a cuff, tumbled into a low spot out of the wind. At some point every burr's journey has to end, doesn't it?

She walked the streets of Montevideo with her city cousins, Chola and ChiChí, in high heels, setting down roots with every step. They shopped and went to the movies on Avenida 18 de Julio, flirted with the dapper men under the palm trees at the Plaza del Entrevero, and joked at the muscular sexual whirlwind of horses and men that was the statue at the center of the park's fountain.

The years passed.

*
* *

Between oblivion and fantasy, memory.

3: Little Cub, Claw Hooks

*
*   *

Joy: the fluid resistance and its giving way.

Each little foot on each pedal sank down and the forward momentum of this bike pushed the foot and pedal back up and an oiled chain glided with the barest clicking and the tires sipped up every crack and contour in the winter-pocked New England asphalt of this plat.

*
*   *

Dream: At some point in my childhood, older than I should have been but still young, Andrés, my cousin four years older than me, and his father (also Andrés), Teresa's husband, taught me to ride on my cousin's bike. All I remember is the day the hand let go of the seat and I continued forward and forward and forward, around the curve of the street and out of sight, down to the schoolyard at the cul-de-sac and back around. For the first time in my little life, no one was watching me. I felt light and yet brimming with exuberance, as if I were a bowl of glowing water sloshing with each bump ready to spill over. I was alone, utterly alone and in control and completely out of control. Little burr caught in someone else's nest, unhooked and flown away.

Instead: In the utility closet of the public housing apartment my mother and I lived in was my own bike with its training wheels on. How could they come off, lest I hurt myself? What kind of a mother was mine? Closely perimetered, watched by neighbor "aunts" and their daughter "cousins" just outside the building's front door, I was allowed to pedal only in a tight circle, the awkwardness of those extra wheels making turns difficult. My face burned, and soon that bike never left that closet. At other boys' sleepovers I prayed no one would pull out their bike and push the handlebars my way. When friends came over, I did everything to make sure the closet door never opened. I was trapped by eyes everywhere. Little burr, grip your story tightly: hold on, hold on.

*
*   *

At forty-seven, what else could it be but a fibroid swelling my mother's mother's belly? But with a little more investigation, behind that tumor lay a child—a miracle or a curse? When this seventh child, Carlos, caught and stuck fast in my grandmother Blanca's tired flesh, my mother found herself caught as well. After the premature birth and Blanca's recuperation in the hospital from surgery to remove the tumor, my mother was called away from high heels and city lights and tinkling elevators and young men in cheap suits and polished shoes. She returned to her childhood at twenty-eight, returned to a newborn child—mere wisp of a congealed life with the most fragile matchsticks for limbs—in need of a mother. Returned and mothered her brother.

*
*   *

Philanthropium, "man-lover," for the characteristic "love" of its
burrs for any passerby

"Like cures like": gravelly burdock seeds ground down will likewise grind away and dispel stony grievances lodged in all the soft cul-de-sacs of the body.

When I was seven, another boy and I would hide in a fort of bedsheets and chairs. I would hitch my pajamas down, and he would rub himself in the crack of my soft buttocks. His skin was darker, Indian caramel, and I pressed my pale little cock against his ass and we were two small hooks, hanging together off the underside of loneliness.

He and I were lost in the softness of each other when my mother entered my bedroom and demanded to know what was going on under the sheets of our fort. When she pulled them back she was horrified. There was the rough grab of the arm and the hasty hiking up of pajama bottoms. The other boy stayed in my room while she dragged me down the dark hallway to her own room for the rest of the night.

For years, I slept in my mother's bed every night, until at nine years old I finally refused.

*
* *

Because when no one will tell you, and you suspect that when you are distracted they are passing your life from hand to hand behind their backs, what else can you do but imagine* possibilities? When roots are tenuous, seeds proliferate—each a terrible fiery world—waiting for a drop of water.

("You've got this all wrong.
This is not how any of this happened,"
all the ghosts say.)

* It made perfect sense. At my Catholic elementary school I was teased mercilessly for my nose (and underneath that, I also always feared, for my foreignness**). After the episode of the swastika during the Uruguay visit, it all became clear to me. Now I understood that I was, secretly, Jewish. Though in my very Catholic little world in Rhode Island I had never met anyone Jewish, I was convinced this was the key to the

mystery of my difference and the mystery of the father I had never known.

(*"*You've got it all wrong.
This is not how any of this happened,"
my grandparents say.)

** They all told me my father's name was Donald Wilkinson, the strangeness of this thoroughly un-Spanish name resolved by the immigrant nature of his immigrant family. He must have been the eldest son of the Jewish family my mother worked for in Montevideo. He stole glances,*** and she returned them. Unable to appease his family mortified by his blood-betrayal or even consider her father, petit fascist in his tin-roofed shack with one son Adolfo, another Franco, and later on that dog named Pinochet, they fled, hooked to each other, and landed in Rhode Island where the little seed they shared sprouted.

(*"*You've got it all wrong.
This is not how any of this happened,"
[my father would say].)

*** There was once a photograph tucked into the frame of the mirror in my childhood bedroom, and then one day it disappeared. My father: a serious, stern-faced man standing against a railing that looks out over a great atrium. Behind: incongruously and improbably, a giant Tyrannosaurus rex grinning his toothy laugh and waving his little paws. Donald Wilkinson's hair was thick and waved in tight curls;

tufts of chest hair puffed out of the open collar of his shirt on his olive skin. Obviously Sephardic: from Spain by way of the Canary Islands. Hello Donald, hello Tyrannosaurus rex. Good-bye.****

("You've got it all wrong.
This is not how any of this happened,"
my mother says.)

**** Too bad none of it is true. Not Jewishness, nor forbidden love, nor the name "Donald Wilkinson" pinned on that stern face. Just more weeds.

*
* *

"You're just like your father," my godmother Teresa would tell me whenever I trumped her in some inconsequential debate with my nine-year-old's crafty steel-trap logic. At this I always recoiled and grew mute. He—the Devil—must have been so smart, and I must be so evil for being so smart. She knew how to shut me up (though now I know she was trying to pry open my mouth: *Ask! Ask! Just once, ask!*).

*
* *

In the spotless white vinyl interior of my mother's little red Volkswagen car I did ask once. I was probably only four years old: when I looked hurriedly away my eyes could barely see out the windows—all I saw were the telephone poles passing by and the empty hard blue sky. "Who is my father?" I only remember jumping over telephone poles in my mind as they sped by. If I jumped high enough, maybe I could get away from her terrifying anger that eclipses to this day any memory of what she actually said in response.

Later, the only other times I ever asked were out of sheer necessity—school forms, standardized tests, college applications—and "Donald Wilkinson" would have to be enough.

*
* *

Love Leaves,
for the wide heart-shaped leaves
or for the brutal truth

After several months, my mother's mother recuperated and emerged from the hospital to return home and resume her role as matron. After several months, how deep do the tiny hooks of an infant dig in? After several months, how painful is the ripping apart? In what strange world does one seed seek shelter in two fruit? None. And so my mother, my youngest uncle's sister-mother, no longer needed, was unceremoniously thrown out of the house and told to fend for herself once again.

Seedless burr, where will you go?

*
* *

Dream: She fled in the night in
the arms of her lover to another
world, a better world.

                              Instead: She was hired as a
                              domestic by a diplomatic family
                              and was carried like an appli-
                              ance to New York, where they
                              exploited her without a second
                              thought.

                                   *
                                 *   *

What does the burr feel when it is ripped free? Tossed into the
brush strange from its own home, estranged from its beginning
and uncertain of its end.

*
* *

Dream: when summer falls to
the ground and autumn winds
sweep up the debris in purging
gales, warty milkweed pods
crack and release their seeds
glowing in blowing silks to the
dance of October storms. Seeds
catch carelessly, without a care,
in high grasses, brambles, wild
curls of his hair on an afternoon hike across a meadow to
get to the woods, in the space
between the nape of his neck
and the collar of his shirt when
an invisible eddy of air col-
lapses like a bubble.

Instead: burdock burr-tight,
burr burning to stow itself away
and pilgrim passage across by
any means necessary. Does not
care who is left behind, what it
takes, when news gets back,
where the waves wash ashore,
why the crossing completes
itself, how much hooks can
hurt. What should this cargo
care, carrying its own hidden
freight, its very own?

```
*   *   *   *   *   *   *   *   *   *   *   *   *   *   *   *   *   *   *   *   *   *   *
  *   *   *   *   *   *   *   *   *   *   *   *   *   *   *   *   *   *   *   *   *   *   *
    *   *   *   *   *   *   *   *   *   *   *   *   *   *   *   *   *   *   *   *   *   *
      *   *   *   *   *   *   *   *   *   *   *   *   *   *   *   *   *   *   *   *   *
        *   *   *   *   *   *   *   *   *   *   *   *   *   *   *   *   *   *   *   *
          *   *   *   *   *   *   *   *   *   *   *   *   *   *   *   *   *   *   *
            *   *   *   *   *   *   *   *   *   *   *   *   *   *   *   *   *   *
              *   *   *   *   *   *   *   *   *   *   *   *   *   *   *   *   *
                *   *   *   *   *   *   *   *   *   *   *   *   *   *   *   *
                  *   *   *   *   *   *   *   *   *   *   *   *   *   *   *
                    *   *   *   *   *   *   *   *   *   *   *   *   *   *
                      *   *   *   *   *   *   *   *   *   *   *   *   *
                        *   *   *   *   *   *   *   *   *   *   *   *
                          *   *   *   *   *   *   *   *   *   *   *
                            *   *   *   *   *   *   *   *   *   *
                              *   *   *   *   *   *   *   *   *
                                *   *   *   *   *   *   *   *
                                  *   *   *   *   *   *   *
                                    *   *   *   *   *   *
                                      *   *   *   *   *
                                        *   *   *   *
                                          *   *   *
                                            *   *
                                              *



                                              *
                                            *   *
```

[Farther Father]

"The other looks for him under the earth"

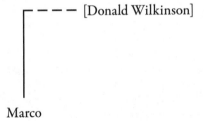

[Donald Wilkinson]

Marco

[Taxonomy:
Genus:
Wilkinson]

Wilkinson: a box, a screen. a hollow sphere, a steady plume of
smoke. an unflattering blemish or scar. a question.

For twenty-one years I thought this was my inheritance. His
name was Donald. His was the name I didn't write in the Father's
Day card I didn't make as the rest of my third-grade class cray-
oned and pasted devotion to their patriarchs. For me there were
only mute, stuttering sobs racking through me and a perplexed
teacher who realized too late to save me from embarrassment.

And all of this for a phantom: my trauma misplaced, mis-
directed, misunderstood.

Countless school forms and applications, even college applications, were occasions for a strange ritual: the awkward approach,
the quiet and unconvincingly nonchalant request of my mother
for this one piece of information. "What is my father's name?"
and then the quick retreat.

"Donald Wilkinson." "Donald Wilkinson." "Donald Wilkinson." "Donald Wilkinson." "Donald Wilkinson." "Donald Wilkinson." Always the same answer: this criminal act, this lie.

"Is he living or is he dead?"

The most basic questions became labyrinths, the answers minotaurs, misshapen.

[This Plain-Sight Treasure: Some Rules for Foraging in Waste Spaces]

Ramp Season (cornelian cherry flowers sulfur the snow; horse-chestnut leaves emerge from sticky sepals brown and pleated; trout lilies; willow wands bristle chartreuse; Dutchman's breeches)

1. Look for the green robe of the forest, bright across the hills by streams.

2. Loosen sashes, undo buttons, tie hair up so the gelid air and the warm press of the sun meet at your neck. Cry at this sweet return.

3. Below the green, the purple bruise that runs to ground. *[Remember the harm you cause in this world.]* With each pull, the pungent smell of tears, the smell that you relish.

4. There is always more than enough. There is always. More means enough is just. Just enough. Means giving up the last little bit back. There is always more than enough.

5. One out of ten once every ten years is enough.

6. Don't forget that you owe this much: to return in the dwindling fall to find brittle wands filled with black seeds, to scatter them widely and wish increase.

7. Don't forget that you owe this much: *[Each son that seedlings from your hand is now yours.]*

Garlic Mustard Season (bright-yellow turnip flowers; violets stitched through turf; daylilies fountain green)

1. Don't despise anything. This bitterness is your mother and this rampage is your father pervading everywhere.

2. The eye sees itself. When one hand meets another, which is the one touching? Open your mouth to the possibility that you are this sound exploding across the universe, these white flowers, these seeds inevitably sown.

3. Imagine a clean world. Imagine Euclid. Imagine proof of the mind's architecture. Imagine the border. Imagine the present as the end of history. *[Imagine your life never invaded by a son.]* All imagined.

4. Eat this plant as if it were the rarest, most precious prize. *[Be voracious in your love]* for it *[me]*. Hold nothing back until nothing is left of you or the world.

5. Remember when harvesting this plant from the soil, roots and all, that the absence of one allows for the presence of another. *[Consider your son.]* Consider what your eventual absence will allow.

Japanese Knotweed Season (redbud blossoms the size of ball bearings; winter cress inflorescences tight like little broccolis; chickweed flowers, five rabbit-eared petals little noticed)

1. Remember *Alien*. Respect that which has the power to overtake you and your world. *[Remember, fathers get eaten by their sons, from the inside out.]*

2. Swallow every last bite lest the remainder take root and swallow you in turn.

3. Come to terms with sweetness as the heart of destruction.

4. Understand karma as a collective phenomenon, collecting along stream banks in public parks, *[as a toy underfoot in a relative's house to remind you,]* behind the guardrail of the cloverleaf, in a pickling jar in your refrigerator or as compote on your ice cream.

Serviceberry Season (sweet potato slips; melon seedlings; cattails swell on pond edges and in ditches)

1. Eat while you are picking: become friendly with your quarry.

2. Don't be too thorough: share with the birds and with those who will come after you. *[Your hidden son will always be right behind you.]*

3. Don't worry about the ones that fall on the ground: share a meal with the mice, voles, and other ground-dwellers who wouldn't otherwise reach these berries high in the air.

4. Don't worry about the ones that fall on the ground: *[Your hidden son will always be right behind you.]*

5. Share with friends: there is always more than enough.

6. Share with strangers: *[Your hidden son will always be right behind you.]*

Linden Flower Season (Saint John's wort blooms bright yellow, bleeds deep purple; straw hat, wide brim; lettuce rockets sunward)

1. Breathe deeply: sit under a linden tree in bloom and be enveloped in fragrance once thought to halt epileptic seizures.

2. Consider scent. The *Lotus Sutra* describes other universes (populated by other beings just like you) made entirely of fragrance. *[Your hidden son: just like you, in another universe.]*

3. Don't be too thorough: there is always more than enough. *[Your hidden son will always be right behind you.]*

4. Notice . . . the surprising number of insects that are the exact shade of creamy chartreuse as the flowers. *[Notice . . . his hair is just like yours, his eyes pierce just like yours, his refusal to smile just like . . .]*

5. Fill your bag with the little spangled dry flower clusters, each only faintly fragrant, and then tie it shut. *[How long did the memory of his scent last after you closed the door?]*

6. Fifteen minutes later, open the bag and feel the moist air inside, from where? *[Even now, can you untie your thoughts and feel his softness fill you?]*

7. Peer into the bag and breathe deeply. The fragrance—citrus, jasmine, rot—overwhelms, pacifies, lulls.

Wheat and Garlic Season (work in the early hours, sleep at noon; days shorten, autumn already on your mind; search for turnip seeds in old shoeboxes)

1. Everything is wild. Acknowledge that *[all things have their own life]*, completely interdependent but also completely independent of your own, and then even food *[planted by your own hand]* is wild.

2. Harvesting is foraging, foraging is harvesting. Seeing the wheat *[seeing you back]* is foraging. Seeing all food as your food *[wherever it may be]* is harvesting.

3. There is always more than enough. Consider the gleaners: on two legs, on four legs, on six, on none. *[Your hidden son is always right behind you.]*

4. Find joy in interdependence: how the wheat wrapped around wheat makes a shock, how heads of garlic are held up off the ground by the green stems of others to cure in the summer sun.

Wild Apple Season (winter wheat sown; goldenrod and aster brocade the fields)

1. Perhaps property is best conceived of as a unit of use instead of a unit of space and time.

2. Notice . . . lost in a hedgerow on the side of a country road, apples tumble into your eyes and how could you refuse them? *[How could you refuse me?]*

3. Your eyes are like five-gallon buckets. Fill them up. *[How could you refuse me?]*

4. Wormholes are an invitation to sit down at the same table to the same meal. Be a gracious guest and accept the pulled-out chair. *[How could you refuse me?]*

5. There is always more than enough. *[How could you refuse me?]*

6. A week later, when you drive along the same road and see a woman busily collecting from the same tree, from *your* tree, remember there is always more than enough. *[How could you refuse me?]*

7. And then look away *[How could you refuse me?]*, and see on the other side of the road *[How could you refuse me?]* the thirty pounds of bright orange-and-yellow shelves of chicken-of-the-woods mushroom pouring out of a splintered hunk of a tree stump. It pours into your eyes. *[How could you refuse me?]*

Wild Grape and Crabapple Season (asparagus, golden; afternoons bend toward night; season of regrets for things unaccomplished)

1. Hitching, there they are on the side of the road you drive on every day. You've seen them for at least a month. Stop and pick them up. *[Pick me up.]*

2. Consider how very much like blood grape juice is as you press it and it runs thick and black down your forearms. You press and you wring and the skinned boundaries break: this sacrifice, this one being, this streaming extravagance. *[Pick me up.]*

3. There is always more than enough. *[Pick me up.]*

4. Soften *[No one will see.]* . . . crabapples ping hard, like stones into the bucket; roll soft like ruptured golden eyeballs in the

boiling water; strain viscous and pink like the unseen imagined smooth walls of your gut, pouring into the bowl of your hips, curdling into intestines, and setting into kidneys, liver, heart.

5. As the liquid boils into jelly and vapor coats the kitchen windows, lament the loss of the hearth as an architectural cornerstone. Had you had it, this pot could sit over embers or hang over licking tongues, and the whole house *[They will never notice.]* huddled close against cold could cook: stories told, songs sung, lessons taught, mysteries mulled into one solid, translucent belly, hipped by flagstones, ribbed by stone walls, capped by a throat of brick singing smoky songs into the chill and darkening rare twilight air of autumn.

6. Notice how unnoticed you are *[No one will see.]* . . . you and your friends *[They will never notice.]* on the side of the busy throughway with your five-gallon buckets collecting crabapples and wild grapes. *[Pick me up.]* How much do you weigh in the bucket of the world's attention? *[How could you refuse me?]* Go on inconspicuous *[No one will see!]*, picking at the edges of the unseen *[They will never notice!]*, gorging, satisfied and joyous *[Pick me up!]* in the slips and oversights of a busy world. *[Please!]*

Mater

"María Landó, María Landó, María Landó,
María Landó sólo trabaja,
María Landó sólo trabaja,
María Landó sólo trabaja
María Landó sólo trabaja
y su trabajo es ajeno."

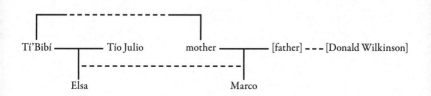

Flower: Madder

Galium verum, L.
Rubia tinctorum, L.

Madder, from Old English, *mædere,* "dye plant," life which
    stains, ruinous marvel, a lie alloyed to a truth

"No se puede tapar el sol con las manos."

/

"You can't hide the sun with your hands."

1: Cradle-Cleave

>
<
>

Cleavers, from the hooks that cause it to stick to anything

In the garden a tangle of whirling green stars climbs over any-thing and everything on slender stems barbed everywhere with tiny hooks. Anything to get higher and out of the thicket to the sun. To be the sun, to lord over the others more privileged, to be desired over those more proper to this ground: explosions of sulfur-yellow flowers, bombs of jealousy, clouds of dazzling anger brocaded into the sky. Trace the maze of clawing aspiration down and it all converges to one rough, bloody root. The gardener passes by, and with one tug the whole empire wilts away.

>
<
>

They were tireless in those early days, transplants in a new field hastening to seed. During the day my aunt Tí'Bibí worked in the textile factory, one more bobbin of thread spinning its life out among the thick rubber belts speeding through the green metal machines, their heady volatile molecules vaporizing and filling the atmosphere of the cavernous shop floor. For the second shift from three to eleven p.m., my mother took her place. In the eve-nings my aunt knitted with clacking golden metal needles or worked her own 1970s loom, rows and rows of shiny metal toggles and the shuttle that swept from side to side, with her tod-dler daughter on the plush couch by the kerosene stove watching TV and fondling the clouds of soft yarn bundled in a basket. And though I would not arrive for several months, perhaps my ghost already lingered, a future memory: I, the other child, quiet and hiding in the corner behind the couch, looking through the pile of newspaper circulars at men tightly packaged in pure white cotton in Fruit of the Loom ads.

One afternoon in the twilight between day and night when cousins crossed paths, my mother cornered my aunt.

"I'm pregnant, and I can only have it if you take care of it."

> >
> <
> >

("You've got it all wrong.")

> >
> <
> >

When my mother fled her abusive Uruguayan employers in New York for Rhode Island, she landed among cousins who had emigrated before her from Uruguay: Bibí, who, when confronted with either abetting an abortion or fostering a baby, agreed to take me into her home; and Teresa, whose son Andrés was like an older brother to me and whose husband, also Andrés, was like the father I never had, who treated me with disinterest at best.

Little root swept up and lodged in a crack in the ground, is it survival, spite, jealousy, or anger that speeds your determination? Reach up, climb over, wind around and overpower. Whatever her cousins achieved, my mother was resolute in matching. Living room sets, hutches, plates to fill hutches, children.

> >
> <
> >

Though he wasn't my father, there really was a Donald Wilkinson. He married this poor immigrant, factory worker, and maid for her money. He showed up at the appointed time and place, that a deal might be made and his nationality conferred upon her. If she could become American then she in turn could make the man who would be my real father an American as well.

Donald Wilkinson: ghost-father, certificate-father, typed shadow across my life.

>
<
>

("This is not how any of this happened.")

>
<
>

Mother Mary, handmaid, bird-catcher, your body a weave of grasping stars reaching up to replace the sun with your own. Birth him and then cut yourself down, cradle him in the scratching arms of your own martyrdom. Teach him to reach for little, that his portion is meager: a cloud of minute ocher flowers in a cave instead of one limitless sun in a limitless sky.

>
<
>

Handmaid, maid with scalded hands, cracking hands, hands wrapped around steel wool, hands plunged into toilet bowls and sinks of greasy water and cat litter boxes, hands too busy, hands too angry, hands that cover the sun and whose shadow falls like a black bird, fingers outspread like wings, over your son. The only embrace they will ever offer.

> >
> <
> >

What I remember: After school we go to a different house every day. Irene's desk piled high and messy with accounting work. Bob's office of dark wood paneling and the lawyer's boxes that match. Belle's opulent apartment, sinister and vibrating with polished brass and glints of gold. Elizabeth's autumnal backyard with the shining birches and the high meadow grasses dried golden in the back, spiders building webs, ants on their way. I ask my mother repeatedly if I can help her in some way so she can be done sooner and we can finally go home: vacuum the den, polish the coffee table. Every time she says, "No."

What I forget: A Baskin-Robbins sundae on a weekday evening after finishing up at Irene's. Chicken sandwiches slick and greasy in their shiny silver-and-red foil wrappers from Wendy's on the way home from Belle's. The hamburgers bubbling in pools of gray fat in the pan on Shirley's stove in the middle of the day on Saturday for my lunch, in between cleaning the bathroom and vacuuming the living room.

>
<
>

When my mother was far along in her pregnancy, months after my true father—fourteen years older than her, divorced, uninterested in starting a second family—had left her amid accusations of entrapment and deception, he ran into her at the mall.

"Veo que seguís con esta locura." (I see you're going through with this craziness.)

And kept walking.

>
<
>

("You've got it all wrong")

>
<
>

"If anyone ever asks, don't ever tell them I clean houses," she said, leaving me suddenly grasping at a million petty barbed lies to rally a seven-year-old life around the lacunae of afternoons and weekends spent in secret houses, reading books curled up in strange chairs, humming in tune with the vacuum to try and shut it out. My mother was a maid.

>
<
>

What is the natural fruit at the end of a life spent scrambling to the sky? What little boy doesn't wonder if he might not in fact be the Second Coming?

>
<
>

Galium, from Greek, *gala,* for "milk."
Renning, for its ability to curdle milk.

That other Mother's belly grew taut like a drum and the skin cracked into shining silver webs. Her breasts swelled and grew sore. Her nipples flowered into moons. Her neighbors looked away, or worse looked ahead and through, or worst looked at her with stones in their eyes.

Even now, so close, she manages the milking, and later when she goes out of her house it is always in the hottest part of the white afternoon when others sleep. Up the flinty hill along the worn path, the straw of her sandals smashes the wild thyme down. The smell makes her dizzy on the switchbacks. Up among the scrub, tangled in the branches that scratch her bare arms, she finds the ladder of herb, its prickly leaves whorling along the stems that clamber up through the shrubs. In her mother's great wooden mortar, whose bowl has grown soft and furred with the use of generations, the stems and the leaves will give up their bitter green juice to the heavy-breathed pounding, the patient drop and twist of the pestle.

Tiny sickle, no bigger than her thumb: her little friend, her only company, pulled from the swaddling of the doubled-over worn linen of her robe where she's learned to keep it close. She leans forward, ready to be scratched by the herb as she reaches with her left hand and swipes with her right, but before she can touch it the herb swells, and in front of her eyes a hundred—a thousand—buds grow fat among the leaves. Catching her breath, she sits back on the sharp stones in the shade of a shrub and looks confusedly from the profusion of tiny golden-yellow flower buds to the growing stains of wetness across her chest.

Back home, before life returns to the streets of the village, she slowly pours the dark green juice from the stems she eventually collected and crushed into the pail of goat's milk from the morning. Stirring clockwise, she waits for the curdled blooms to appear.

> \
< \
>

Root red, flower gold, leaf star, cleavers hold.

> \
< \
>

My mother will forever remember that Mrs. Oden always had a package of Pampers waiting every week when she came to clean the small ranch house in Cranston with its Scandinavian blond wood paneling and the living room that no one ever sat in.

I will always remember the white-vinyl-padded daybed splashed with a sixties flower-graphic print in the breezeway between the dining room and the garage, and the rows of little horizontal glass panes on the front and back doors that louvered open and closed to let air in or to keep it out. I played on the scratchy low-pile carpeting with a deck of cards, trying hard to keep one tilted against another just right to balance. (Always trying to build my house in another's.) I lay on the coolness of the vinyl with a Raggedy Andy doll for company. While my mother cleaned, Mrs. Oden with her dyed-blond hair and her quirky dentured smile and her glasses on a thin chain around her neck would take me out into the backyard where it was always sunny and splash me with a hose and spin the umbrella clothesline like a pinwheel.

>
<
>

I was born on Thursday, July 1, 1976, at 5:01 p.m. at Kent County Hospital in Warwick, Rhode Island, on Toll Gate Road, a spot off the beaten track in a green woodsy dell where a small dairy farm was still the hospital's neighbor. That afternoon, as I screamed my way into the world, black-and-white cows with mud-splattered legs stood in the green-and-brown paddock in a drizzle, chewing their cuds absentmindedly, unknowingly producing milk for some other baby's searching mouth. Soft and kind childless mothers, will you pay my passage with my weight's-worth of milk in a shiny bucket, that I might pass through the threshold into this land?

>
<
>

"It's important that you know he was there when you were born," a relative tells me one day, insistently, as if to impress that he did try even if he failed. My father's presence at my birth is something I only learn about well into my thirties. This story is still unfinished, dripping and spilling across decades of my life.

>
<
>

Our Lady's bedstraw, from the legend that this was the plant that
formed the bedding in Christ's cradle

*Why would you lay the slick, purple, mewling body of a new-
born against those rough stems, with their back-curved spines
and leaves covered in prickling hairs? This herb that ladders its
way up to the sky with its million tiny barbs, each prick a step
closer to heaven. She softly uncradles him, lays his head down
against the wilting greenery. In an instant a profusion of golden
flowers springs from the goldening stems and fragrant clouds of
incense fill the air. Little boy, still uncircumcised and uncove-
nanted, scratched by the bed you lie down in, already reaching
up for a father.*

>
<
>

In the end, as I only recently learned, his conscience, family pressure, some faint, half-felt dream impinging on the borders of his
mind asking to be realized: who knows why my father came back
after walking away? From my wailing entrance in early July to
that other Boy's celestial-trumpeted plummet into mortality in
late December, how many times did my father hold me? How
many times was he allowed?

   She was fierce in her protectiveness, having loved a boy and
lost before. By day I was kept close, and each night I was laid in
my aunt's arms rather than his. So how could it surprise anyone

that on that other One's birthday, when his Father dropped him into the scratching cradle of this world to fend for himself, my father stepped out for cigarettes and never returned, leaving this little sulfur-yellow flower behind. Inconsequential thing, a weed, sick and tired of the scratches that came with it.

>
<
>

("This is not how any of this happened.")

>
<
>

2: Hand-Maid

>
<
>

Unlike the biting fragrance of mint—sharpest when fresh—bedstraw, madder, sweet woodruff, and their kin only come into their own when dead. They dry to gold, releasing the soft smell of fresh-mown hay so characteristic of coumarin, the compound they share in common.

>
<
>

What is an un-memory, thing not unknown?
olvido: wormhole of history, unit of oblivion, degree of injury
threads us all
father forget this other son
mother forget that other son
son forget or else
the whole fabric will flame

> >
> <
> >

Memory: Two of my mother's "houses" were at the Royal Crest apartments, a collection of white-plaster and exposed-oak-beam Tudor-style buildings set in a green and idyllic sweep of gentle curves and sunshine, with little bridges over streams and a lake at its center. After my mother finished sweeping, mopping, polishing, sweating, cleaning up, she took me to the lake's edge with a bag of old bread (ours or the casually thrown-out loaf of one of her clients) to feed the geese that congregated there, eager to snap at the fingers of a five-year-old.

> >
> <
> >

Because my older cousin Andrés couldn't say "Tía Bibí" as a toddler, struggling over the sibilant syllables of his mother's sister's name in a land of curled *r*'s and punctuated *b*'s and *d*'s, she became "Tí'Bibí" and my mother, his madrina/godmother, became "Ina." And so in turn, like an echo, my own voice called out "Ina" to

Andrés's mother and "Tí'Bibí" to the woman who was my mother's cousin and my other mother, the one who potty trained me in the late afternoon light of an upper room in her little house, and who now wanders in the corners of my memory, a beneficent pear-shaped matronly ghost with salt-and-pepper hair and a kindly soft smile.

By the kerosene stove with a pot of water on top humidifying the living room, I used to sit as she waved her hand back and forth over her mechanical loom, laying down lines of color. I played with coils of elastic-weave fabric brought home from the factory where she and my mother alternately worked, rolling and unrolling them again and again for the pleasure of the texture under my fingers and the faint smell of rubber that came off them, the same smell at the factory where my mother even then was toiling among the speeding belts and blurring bobbins.

>
<
>

The weedy roots of *Galium verum,* like the cultivated *Rubia tinctorum,* yield a dye long used to create colors ranging from palest pink to deep bloody-brown. The blackish rough skin is scraped back to reveal a bright orange-red core, and this provides a number of compounds, the most important of which is alizarin. Tinting is the same as tainting, the difference being the degree.

>
<
>

Looking for the unseen just means looking for the things you do not want to see: the things that web your chosen world, that wed you to what you choose (or have had chosen for you) to forget.

Roaming through the Catskills woods after a summer storm, we fanned out alone or in pairs or in threes, our eyes cast down among the leaf litter. Fungus connects with its waxy white web of hyphae to birches or pines or beeches. Ladders through itself, birch with birch and beech with beech, making a single tree out of a forest.

Every tree is more dead than alive, every cell of wood a hollowed-out husk, a tiny splinter of bone. Each tree is a bone hung together by mycelia into one body.

>
<
>

Tí'Bibí and Tío Julio had left Uruguay and arrived in Rhode Island on an agricultural fellowship several years before my mother's own circuitous journey brought her there. Tío lived in a bar down the street called Borowski's; Tí'Bibí lived at home in a little two-story Cape Cod with a backyard, where she pinned clothes to a line and tended her ample garden. Each in their own way was a ghost, pale-white figures passing through the world. Along with suitcases, they brought with them a daughter, coffee skin and long black hair, energetic and rebellious, conspicuous counterpoint to their white skin and pallid routines.

Tí'Bibí used to take her daughter's black-and-white guinea pig, Señorita, out of the aquarium tank that stood on a small table by the bathroom and place her plump little quivering body in the backyard under a tipped-over laundry basket so that Señorita could nibble on grass and get some fresh air.

What is cast away is picked up. What blows through the air sinks into the sea. Wound that bleeds is swaddled and tended. The lost are found, one way or another, and cradled.

Who knows why she never told her daughter that she was adopted?

Who knows why she agreed to my mother's proposition?

> >
> <
> >

Xylem cells flow water through their bodies, hollowed out, up to heaven on a wooden ladder. Each one ripens to death and hollowness, collaborating in plumbing the way through sacrifice. In each tree, each beech, maple, oak, and birch, each pine, plane, cedar, and ash, is a cross. From soft green to stiff gold, they drink storms and drizzles and fog and unseen aquifers of water, drop by sticking drop, like so many stitches of a pure-white winding cloth. Lift up the curtain, raise up the cross.

> >
> <
> >

Tap the flesh of the desert myrrh tree with a spearing blaze across its side and fragrant pearls of resin will well up in the gash. The hardened, deep-yellow milky "tears" are collected each week and the wound reinflicted.

Pine, too, cries bouquets in the close green of the woods— the trunk to the side of the path, felled last year but never milled, weeps—but gets closer to heaven once a year, when its gold-green pollen, in exhalations of prayer from Appalachian

mountaintops, sweeps hundreds of miles out over the unfath-
omable sea. Finally settling on the surface, the grains of gold
vanish in a bubbling frenzy of millions of feeding fish mouths,
knit into oily flesh disappearing behind the curtain of the swirling dark waters.

>
<
>

*When that other Mother was herself a child, immaculate, no stain
of red yet or ever, before she was trusted to spin the shuttle through
the shed, her own mother had her sit by her side and scrape the madder roots of their rough, black skin to the bright flesh beneath. With
her mother's eyes fixed on the fell of the loom before her, furtively at
first and then with abandon, the girl chewed on the smaller scarlet
nubs of stiff flesh. She relished the bitterness, that sharp tonic punch.*

*Later she always kept a bit of red root ready to calm the fussy
teething of her own Child, who seemingly carried in his reddening
bones the same bitter yearning.*

[In the corner another child, the other son, coils and uncoils
fabric, lost in the colors, oblivious to the bitter taste dropping
from the One's tongue into his own bones.]

>
<
>

One Friday, while my mother was cleaning the kitchen or scrubbing a toilet somewhere else in this house, Elizabeth and I sat in

the silent gloom of her living room, the curtains all drawn and the lights turned off. She didn't speak or watch TV or knit or read, and so neither did I, her little aping dwarf of a witness. She explained in a hushed and patient tone that Jesus had been crucified on this day and during the hours he hung on the cross we should sit in silence and mourn. And so we sat, she in her armchair and I on her pea-soup-green couch in stuffy mournful repose. I treasured that quiet communion and the solemnity of commemoration. (And what did I think about my mother toiling in light-drenched kitchens and bathrooms during such a time? Didn't she know she was supposed to mourn God's dying? All through my Catholic-school education, my mother was always banging about when all I wanted to do was pray.)

>
<
>

To be clear, she is not here. You will not find her.

Her whole life has shaped her into a María, but she isn't María. Now, her back stoops, curled easily for picking things up off of floors. Now, her ears buzz in perfect canceling counterpoint to the white noise of vacuum cleaners. These days, the cane that steadies her is also adept at pushing things off paths or into place. She is always organizing, always cleaning, always doing, always ignoring what asks her to stop. She is a hurricane spinning into dissipation, expenditure, exhaustion, but here I will not give her a name.

My whole life she has loomed like Mary, awesome and silent, but she isn't Mary. My face turns upward from her lap to the eclipse of her face. My fingers grab at the hem of her shirt in the department store, trying to keep up. Her cross turned into my cross turned into hers again, this telling a crucifixion I should be ashamed of but am not. The littlest salvation is that I will not name her here.

>
<
>

Later that day, Elizabeth and I knelt in the shorter pews of the side aisle of her church, close to the empty and open tabernacle, and I stared into the shining white of the alcove bright as Elizabeth's white hair and the brilliance of the golden tabernacle sparkling like the thin chain that held Elizabeth's glasses, breathed in deep the heaviness of incense in the air, the piercing citrus of polish on the gleaming pale wood of the pews. (Same as the chemical tang of Pledge impregnating my mother's bag of old T-shirt rags carted from house to house.)

>
<
>

("You've got it all wrong.")

>
<
>

3: Bird-Cage

>
<
>

Elsa found a small bird in the backyard, its wing twisted the wrong way, and carried its incredibly light body to her mother. A birdcage was duly purchased, borrowed, or found, and the little bird, "Piru," blue-feathered, black-feathered, white-feathered, hopped on his narrow, delicate, scaly legs along the cage's floor, picking at shiny millet seeds, cracking open the striped shells of sunflower seeds. I was thrilled and disturbed by the softness of Piru's colors and the clicking shiny hardness of the little nails bouncing up and down in my palms, the darting beak and the passionless eyes.

>
<
>

tinctorum, from Latin for "stain."

One can feed small birds in their cages shreds of madder mixed in with their cracked corn, or sunflower seeds, or amaranth— tiny and pearly white or onyx black—and they will easily take it up. Then, when the bruise-black pimpled skin under the plumage has been slipped off and the flesh cleaved away, all kinds of wonders can be read from the reddened, pencil-thin bones.

Ornithometrist, scaling with a loupe at your eye each crimson deposit, do birds like trees fly up in rings too? What auguries do you read in the ornithography of a life held fast for some hidden postmortem purpose? What words emerge from a

stained skeleton thrown up into the air, clattering back down
to earth?

>
<
>

*Later, much later, after all the storm clouds of her life blew through
her and were gone, the old Mother lived her life up in the mountains above Ephesus, quietly clicking one bead against another. She
still kept one goat in the lean-to shed against her small stone hut.
Indomitable, she drove her bones forward up the path, past the
belts of fragrant cedar and shadow that sheltered her home, up to
the open vistas above where the salt of the sea rose in updrafts along
with the eagles that floated up from nowhere, staring. There, in
among the blooming cistus and the rheumatic knobs of olive, she
would find the ladder herb in the thicket, climbing with its minute
barbs to heaven, and cut it down.*

>
<
>

(all the ghosts say)

>
<
>

My mother never had another relationship after whatever it was
that gave birth to me. In her hardness she was virginal. In her
capacity for self-sacrifice she was delusional, blotting out the

obvious sun in the sky with her fingers and judging the work dark for the rest of us. That he was never spoken of meant my father didn't exist. She might furiously climb up in a tangling net of barbs and stony silences and cover the sun, dye the ground blood-red with bitterness and weave a sturdy cage, but I was proof, light spilling through fingers, a little birdsong filtering through, that there once was another, that she was soft and yielding then.

>
<
>

[my father would say]

>
<
>

As a child I once walked into my mother's bedroom to find the closet door open and my mother's rhythmically flexing, arched foot dancing in the middle of the gloom, bright white like a ghost or a bird suspended in flowing flight. I stood staring, silent, disturbed by this fluidity I had never seen before.

>
<
>

One day the white cage swung empty in the summer breeze from the backyard tree in which it hung, the little trap door list-lessly drifting. Elsa screamed. "Piru! What did you do to Piru?" she demanded of her mother.

Piru seemed to have escaped from a cage not shut tightly enough. Testament, apparently, to a miraculous recovery of wing and flight. Kind-eyed Tí'Bibí, who took in what wasn't hers, seeing the inevitable end . . . what did she do? Nestle the shivering form in a shroud of green grasses? Twist the neck so much thinner than the feathers would suggest, until the barely audible snap? Look the other way with the door wide open, the neighborhood cat in the distance? Too strong to stand suffering, too gentle to countenance truth. What little lies spring and diverge, arm themselves into whole worlds, and burst into flower?

Little birds, Elsa and I hopped about in a panic, searching for Piru. Little did we each know then, we were broken-winged ourselves, each alone in our own cages so subtle the white bars faded into the summer haze.

Little door, where could you be?

>
<
>

Once a year the high priest talked with God. But always first he clothed himself in the winding stitches of white smoke exhaled by the tears of myrrh in the brazier, lest he be smote down, and no matter his own confidence, the other priests always tied a rope to his ankle so that they could drag his corpse out of the Holy of Holies if the conversation didn't go well.

>
<
>

"Whenever anyone asks, Donald Wilkinson is your father's name." This is what I was told from kindergarten through high school whenever the formularies of education's bureaucracy required such a space be filled. This, and nothing more.

When I was twenty-one I was lost in a sleep that lasted for three days. Or maybe these were just the final three days of sleep that had lasted a lifetime. When I woke up I stumbled to the phone and called my mother.

"I want to know about my father."

"Why!?! He left us!"

"I want to know about my father."

That's when, for the first time, I learned my father's true name.

>
<
>

(my mother says)

>
<
>

Miles out from anywhere, in that liminal band of ocean long past the last sight of home sinking behind the swells, and long before the murky charts prophesied purchase, the western sky glowed gold in the morning light. They licked their cracked, salt-dimpled lips as first one and then another sailor stopped his appointed chore to ponder the billowing clouds of gold on the wrong horizon, this double-dawn. After some moments where only the whining of the rigging and the slapping of the water against the ship were heard, the first flakes of bright ocher, pine-perfumed, caught in their arm hairs and in their beards. Within an hour they were inside the flowing cloud of fragrant gold dust, lost.

>
<
>

Most of my childhood was spent in other people's houses. I made two tangling circuits that crossed and wound around each other: one into strangers' living rooms, dens, and bedrooms on a weekly basis so that I was familiar as if in relatives' houses (so familiar I thought of these people as aunts and uncles and grandparents when I was very young); the other into relatives' houses, into spare bedrooms that were never quite mine, into family dynamics where I didn't make sense—slipped in like a shadow half-seen in a corner (familiar but never family, not quite).

>
<
>

Lost, a little Columbus, misrecognizing the stars overhead, mistaking the golden dust floating on the horizon for the beckoning shores of heaven. Always heading just off course, steering my boat by the dark light of a missing father's wrong name, by the terrifying light of a mother blazing with the sweat of two and three jobs and a resentment of her cousins whose tenderness captured me.

>
<
>

If I peeled myself down
to my bones would
I find my secret father there?

                                        If I climbed a tree and refused
                                                      to descend
                                        would these hollow bones
                                        burst into golden flowers?

[Father/Fucker]

"Someone hides from someone else
Hides under his tongue"

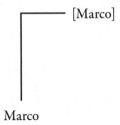

[Marco]

Marco

[Taxonomy:
Species:
Marco]

Marco: a crumbling stone façade. Fluted columns tumbled and
    infilled with dirt and moss. A refrigerator drawer of
    moldering meat. The god of war.

It was like being told you were named after the Devil: a spark
of strange heat, and then suddenly wreathed in dark fire. It was
like being told the name of the curse whose invisible cords had
alternately bound you down and played you like a marionette
your whole life; only, acquiring the name doesn't free you of its
grip—it only snaps tighter.

My whole life I had never met another Marco. Single child
of a single mother—a singular name for a singular child, one of
a kind and mine alone. I often wondered how it must feel for
the unlucky person named John or Tom who had to meet some
not-himself person nearly every day with the same name. How
it must feel to be partial, to have to share identity dispersed

across a world of different experiences in different bodies. But not me. What happened to Marco happened only to me. Does not sharing your name help to cultivate delusions of grandeur? Does every other boy wonder if he is in fact the second coming of his father?

I was twenty-one before I ever learned his name, and so obvious is it in retrospect that I felt stupid to have never guessed it before. Marco, my father: named after the Devil himself, shining hard skin of black volcanic glass, wrapped in sulfurous fumes in the burning furnaces of hell.

Perhaps it does not condemn me so much as it indicts my mother, that even as he left her behind she called out his name and packed it quickly, frantically, like wads of cotton stuffing or gauze, into the bleeding cavity of my little infant chest. "Now you will hold it, and I will hold you, and you will never leave."

("You've got it all wrong.")

[The Way One Thing Touches Itself]

On the other side of the world and decades away from my childhood:

At night as the ferry motors by and its wake swims toward us, the water gleams like oil. Shadows of trees stream with each sliding wave over the nebulous gray of the reflected night, and the bright white houselights from the opposite bank spear in glimmers through the slick black.

~

My skin still floats in oil from my Ayurvedic massage earlier this afternoon, the first of our stops on this Kerala backwater houseboat trip in southern India. Three palm-leaf huts sat by the side of the green water, the smiling masseurs waiting. In the dark of the first hut he poured oil like honey in dribbles on my thighs. He rubbed it like fire into the soles of my feet. His fingers rolled like waves, relentless from hip to ankle, and each time, my boat swayed as his knuckles brushed against my balls or against their wiry hairs, alert like antennae. From the beginning it was inevitable, this innocent erection. How could such electric surges not telegraph and broadcast themselves?

I knew something was up when his fingers ran rings around my nipples, his hands kneaded my pecs like balls of dough, his crotch pressed itself into my hand, limp on the table's side.

~

Out of nowhere the houseboat pitches and rolls with an unseen wave. Moored at the shore for so long, we hardly remember that this craft floats on water, a wick on a bed of oil, waiting to be lit.

~

"So cute," he says softly. I open my eyes and he is looking at me, his mouth curled up in a sly, conspiratorial smile. I chuckle and say, "Thank you," half out of politeness, half out of surprise, and another mysterious half out of relaxing into the table. He bends down and kisses me on the forehead before kissing me on the lips before pouring his tongue into my mouth.

~

Water hyacinth skirts the mirror surface of the canal in the morning, leaves pontooned by bubbles of air held in the plants' own bellies. Breathe in, and hold. The sky-painted water hiccups with ripples first here, then there, and then three feet away, a frenetic haphazard flurry across seconds. Small silver fish kiss the limit line of the world, in love with the danger of drowning in the too-thin ether of air. Circle of mouth, circle of sky; open: let all your life out, let all your life in.

~

By now the massage table is slick with oil, so when he asks me to turn over onto my stomach, I slide easily. The oil and the table and my own erection feel good, a warm aliveness drowsy and sensitive at once.

~

In the middle of the canal in the middle of the night, a small orange fire doubles itself in the water. Silently, the oar paddled by one man barely rippling the dark, a small narrow boat moves toward us, moored on the bank. At the front another man sits next to a white cloud of netting, and between the two in the center of the boat is the small fire, turning them and the boat into thick shadows moving slowly against the black of the water.

~

His hands work continuously in long sweeps across the backs of my legs, my buttocks, my back, my shoulders. After a time, lost between wakefulness and sleep, I lose track: are those his hands or ripples of oil lapping against the banks of my skin?

~

The nightboat slides closer, and I can see the man in front parceling his cloud of net into the water, precisely and with efficient delicacy slipping the white into the black and with arched fingers setting small buoys out without a ripple. How like the waiter in Delhi, setting plates on the table quickly but with graceful concentration, the merest hush of air exhaled between china and linen; or like the chai-wallah in Mussoorie, who proffered the thick milky spiced tea in its tiny cut-glass cup with both hands as if it were the smallest of birds or a newborn child or a jewel, his pinkies extended; or like the men here in Kerala, who with gleaming skin rippling over smooth muscle and blackest of black mustaches, casually hold one corner of their saffron or teal or pink ankle-length lungis up in one hand between thumb and forefinger, the other three fingers arched out like sparrows' wings, as they walk the streets of Kochi or the winding banana lanes of Alappuzha or the jute-sturdied embankments of these backwaters.

Buoying on the surface, clouds merging with water, the way one thing touches itself: all these bodies contacting without a sound.

~

The heavy pour of oil falls from his fingertips held high above my tailbone. For an open moment there is just the sensation of gravity pressing the oil on this one point. I can almost feel the whisper of air across the skin of the oil as if it were my own skin, the nerves of my body climbing up the ladder of oil to his fingers.

When the moment closes, his fingers descend into the oil, into me, effortlessly. Small circle, little fish mouth kissing at the limit of self, opening, caught on a hook, burning in a net of water, squirming to be free or to be caught entirely.

Madder

"Como una estatua de alas que se dispersan por la ciudad"

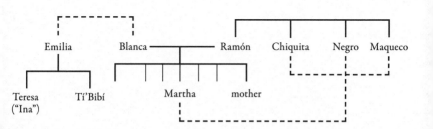

Seed: Shepherd's Purse

Capsella bursa-pastoris, L.

Shepherd's purse, from the seedpods shaped like satchels, shaped
like hearts

*So many as to be invisible in their plentitude, these tiny trod-
den cresses populate pastures and lawns and curbs. Pastor, pasture-
tender, combing each blade of grass back into place, starring each
rosette of sharp leaves across the field. Shepherd, roaming the hills
week after week, what do you carry in that purse? As little as possible, just enough to carry on, to outlive oneself and propel the
future into the future. A handful of cress and a wand of heart-
shaped seeds.*

1: Bright Fruit, Dark Fruit

θ θ θ

Tí'Bibí's sister was my godmother, Teresa, who was to me only
ever "Ina" (short for *madrina,* other-shore for "godmother,"

talisman for "substitute in case of disaster"). She suffered several miscarriages before she gave light to her only living son, Andrés, and breathed a gyre of fire into his chest. My mother suffered neglect and the crime of having a child placed in her arms and then taken away before she snatched me into the world out of the darkness and never let go.

θ θ θ

As children Andrés and I were the closest things each of us had to brothers, though before us a string of ghosts webbed the air with loss we could not see or comprehend. There were simply two young boys tarring a *Star Wars* action figure to a telephone pole with rubber cement, or threading dried leaves to the air with a magnifying glass and a ray of light honed needle-sharp, or gathering ants from their hills emerging through cracks in the pavement to throw into a backyard spiderweb and watch the catch, the struggle, and the resolve to remain trapped.

θ θ θ

Being the youngest of my cousins meant always being last and coming up short. (Sliding down hills into neighborhoods not yet born, caught on the burrs, a burr caught on their hems.) How could a four-year-old compete with an eight- and a ten-year-old at an Easter egg hunt? Whatever deity laid eggs of happiness for little children to hatch had not thought to leave any for me in the grass or under the flowers, but Elsa and Andrés came back beaming with baskets full of brightly colored futures. Myself, I crumbled into inconsolable tears.

θ θ θ

Where was my mother? Leaning into a giant machine at the textile factory? All I remember was Ina taking my hand firmly and walking me out into the yard for our own little Easter egg hunt and coming upon a clutch under the spruce tree. Did I know she had placed them there especially for me? I only remember her beaming face, and my pride, and my love for her attention at that moment, even if forced, even if only a substitute for real love.

θ θ θ

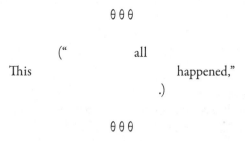

(" all
This happened,"
.)

θ θ θ

There was a Japanese maple tree in one corner of the front yard of Ina's house, sinuous limbs and deep-purple toothed leaves. As kids my cousin Andrés and I would climb into it and cradle in its limbs. We were two fruits hanging in that tree: one the fulfillment of repeatedly dashed hope, bright and sweet; the other the remedy for a hurt displaced across time and space into empty arms, dark and bitter.

θ θ θ

Sometime between my mother's electrocution at one factory and the fantastically colored green hands and blue hair of chemical dye spills at another factory (which is just another way of saying sometime between the time I was seven and eleven), her third-shift work schedule meant I would sleep at Ina's house, a raised ranch at the top of a hill.

What I remember: the faintly peach walls that caught fire in the sunset; creeping into the kitchen, opening up the refrigerator, and wondering what it would be all right to eat; the giant wooden rosary hanging over my godmother and uncle's bed; sitting alone in the living room watching TV; sitting alone in the spare bedroom that was "my" room, reading; sitting alone in the basement, reading; sitting alone on the back deck, reading; watching Ina paint her nails under the light of the living room lamp; watching my uncle watch football on TV; watching my cousin Andrés ride his skateboard in the street from the lifted blinds of the window of the spare bedroom; sitting alone in an empty house, watching Michael Hutchence "slide over here" in slinky hip-hung pants on MTV; watching Andrés's friend Peter, small and blond and on fire like Michael Hutchence, pad down the hall in his pristine tight white underwear to the bathroom during a sleepover; watching the sun set fire to the walls of the house; watching the dust on the living room window light up in the sunset.

θ θ θ

("   all
This   happened,"
                         .)

θ θ θ

What makes a weed: ubiquity. Because omnipresent, troublesome. Because everywhere, where begin? Because universal, forgettable.

When the bitter principle sours the egg, what can follow? Collecting those doomed bequests in a stinking coop so long ago in her family farm childhood, what could my mother hope for?

Was this her dowry from parents who in turn inherited treasures of pain stowed away in the belly of a stowaway in the belly of a boat? Did my mother have to crawl into the coop to retrieve them? And did the door get shut behind her? Because this meanness seems endless, the bitter root dropped into the bones, the bitter juice an endless stream falling through generations—there is no cage and there is only cage. Because omnipresent, troublesome. Because universal, forgettable.

In the summer haze the bars of the cage disappear into the white sky beyond, and we cover the sun with our hands to forget. How can I tell this story when it is only forgetting and when it is only the same thing always and ever? Day after day alone in the summer haze of my childhood, nursing these seeds in my bones, distilling oblivion into crystalline willed forgetting. Now, there seems too little left, too few crumbs to peck at for memory.

θ θ θ

Mother, pour this bitterness into my veins to heal your wounds as your father and your mother did to you. Pour your regurgitated fury into my mouth so hungry for anything and cauterize my little lips into blank song: Who is he? Who is he? Who . . . ? . . . ? . . .

θ θ θ

My grandmother Blanca was herself taken in as a child by others, the Betancor family. And so she and Emilia Betancor grew up as "sisters" under one roof, though I can't help but wonder if she was more servant than sister, more Cinderella than safe. And so Emilia's daughters, Bibí and Teresa, and my mother were "cousins." And so Bibí became my second mother and

Teresa—"Ina"—my third mother: a succession of mothers, a succession of houses, a succession of saving sadnesses.

θ θ θ

Shepherds, slip the skin of lost lambs over orphan shoulders, wool over loss and deny grief by cauling it love. All too sickly, too many children die of cold, of being lost in the flock, mouth separated from teat, of being one too many, of no reason at all, and so this ancient ritual of swapping:

Quick! Quick! With a sharp knife cut the cord, gut the corpse, disrobe the soulless slip of flesh of its coat. Force the shivering orphan into its bloody inheritance, push shaking legs through ragged holes and rub the funk of foreign lanolin into the youngster's face. Pour the other mother's milk across black lips and unknowing tongue, that it might musk the shit and fool the matron: no death has ever happened, no loss was ever had. This is mine and always was, this child is mine and always will be.

In this way the flock pastors its own.

θ θ θ

I was not the first substitution, not the only surrogate love to replace loss, to require care when original mothers were insufficient, when purses ran short and mouths were too many.

My mother's younger sister, Martha, escaped the iron by being sent to live with their spinster aunt, Chiquita, and bachelor uncles Negro, Chiquito, and Maqueco. (Why did they never marry? What were their defects, their unspeakable loves, that left them without seeds to sow?) She left the four-room house at the bottom of the hill by the arroyo that would often flood in the middle of the night, ruining the ill-fated family fields, to live at the top of the hill doted on by four "parents" in her aunt Chiquita's tidy garden of succulents and passionflowers twined through the front gate. She got to go to school. She got to have the boyfriend with the motorcycle. She got to get married and have children and a house and a garden of her own. As far as my mother was concerned, Martha was whisked away to heaven as a girl while she labored in hell, stoking her little iron's heat with embers in its belly.

θ θ θ

Blanca was known for her flower garden, small kingdom of beauty on a farm devoted to survival. She must have dreamed of foxgloves and geraniums and roses among the fields of alfalfa and beans, chicken coops and pig pens, the wash and the children. So what was a daughter but another source of fecundity, another means of production? Better to have sons, productive but also free, seeds that might fly far and wide and come to something, beautiful to look upon and tend.

θ θ θ

To tell this story, what is needed?

In another house, there is Blanca up against
a whitewashed wall.
    In a crowded house, there is my mother cradling a little iron,
                        and then a little brother,
                                and then a suitcase.

In an empty house, there is me with my foot planted
at the curb.

θ θ θ

      ("   all

This   happened,"
                        .)

θ θ θ

Feed a preponderance of shepherd's purse's bitter leaves to chickens and their egg yolks will darken, sometimes to a sickly olive green.

θ θ θ

I had been trained and trained well: always polite, always the right answer, always quiet when quiet was needed. Trained into tight but awkward circles in a parking lot under watchful eyes, this little queer thing, a three-wheeled bicycle teetering and nearly collapsing under the stress of too small a world.

    Take a small space for yourself, grow among the cracks and between the larger herbs. Rosette of bitterness, tenacious roots: wandering is not for you, the sky is not for you, horizon and beyond-horizon not for you.

θ θ θ

Wind-worn, star-brooches, shuttles spinning through the warp and never caught: seeds that never make it, never land in the clasping earth. Where do you? What are you?

2: Ripening to Rot

θ θ θ

Deep in the green, clasped tight in a downward-mouthing cup of matter, a cell differentiates into four siblings. Who can say why only one of these is kept to become a future seed, a future rosette of green, a future stipple of white against the greater pattern, a future heart-shaped purse safeguarding a seed, a future? Does the survivor carry the silhouetted shadows of his own private luck—three soft marks against his fourth?

θ θ θ

Having come with nothing, going was everything, and everything was required.

Five times I have traveled with my mother back to Uruguay, and each time the journey took months. It began in the off-season circling around the chrome orbits of Kmart clearance racks searching for bathing suits in November, heavy jackets in July. Towels, small appliances, bottles of Johnnie Walker wrapped and hidden (three for the uncles, one for customs). A closet of manic kindness, reprisal, obligation, recrimination—filled, sale by sale, for the travels ahead. Trip across hemispheres and seasons, trip to the alternate future of never having left, trip to the past that though left behind could never be escaped.

A month or more before, the suitcases emerged from under the bed, one laid inside the other in an infinite regression of capacity into the smallest parcel, a mustard seed towing in its coat a yellow tower, a thousand children to feed and sustain, the ghost of its own mother that once held it aloft in the wind and threw it away. Each valija (literally "valise," quaint holdover in a held-over world, amber-captured and ever-present-gone) emerged like a molting insect one from another's skin until a family of them was laid out on the floor of my mother's bedroom, ready to be filled.

She filled them first one way and then another, judging and rejudging what would make it in and who would receive what. This coat for this niece, those pants for that nephew, that cream for an aunt, and always the bottles of Johnnie Walker for the uncles. The suitcases would overflow with beneficence (and this, just the smaller movables. Beyond the laden suitcases were also the washer and dryer for the sister, the medical-school education for the niece), and she would show them all what she could produce. I walked into the room and watched, mystified. She looked up at me and smiled.

θ θ θ

(" all
This   happened,"
.)

θ θ θ

Seed or purse to hold it in: each seed a purse clasped shut, clasped close, lips pursed lest this life fly.

θ θ θ

Instead of one sandwich, two. Instead of two sandwiches, two stuffed with bloody roast beef and mayonnaise until their bellies bulged and the bread was damp mush.

My mother was obsessively fixated on feeding her own privation by forcing me to eat for the little girl hunched over her iron.

Yet I have no memory of her ever hugging me except in greeting, nor of telling this little hologram of herself/her little brother-son/her lover, "I love you."

Instead, a distant aunt of mine nicknamed China, rotund sphere of kindness whose kids went to the same elementary school as me, would come by my table in the cafeteria on the days she volunteered as a lunch monitor and, seeing my anguish at having finished one sandwich but still having a whole other one in front of me, would ask with her smiling eyes and her tinkling accent, "Are you all done with your lunch?" I nodded nervously, knowing that the nuns who ran our parochial school would yell at us to never waste food, and she erased all my troubles with one clean whisk of a hand lifting sandwich, wrapper, and brown paper bag in an arc into the nearby garbage can.

Oh largeness of the generosity that takes away, that makes things vanish, that blesses smallness with smallness!

θ θ θ

After getting lost in the skin-tight white spandex of Axl Rose on the TV in the living room of an otherwise empty house that was not mine and whose true inhabitants were all somewhere else in their own lives, I found myself, unbidden, out on the front lawn of Ina's house staring up into the summer sunset sky and out down Deerfield Road at the top of a hill. Out to the west where orange and amethyst and a curious unrecognizable turquoise flamed and dampened and subsided in some other place I wanted to be.

There was no one in the house to look out the window and wonder at this strange boy's wonder. There was no neighbor or neighbor-kid. There was no hold, but my feet never left the curb.

θ θ θ

Shepherd's purse's bitter juice is effective in the binding up of all wounds, external or internal. In World War I, the Germans used it to treat their wounded; the Allies stuffed sphagnum moss into gaping wounds when bandages ran out; coconut water, naturally sterile, dripped into intravenous lines, slipping from one enclosed seed into another.

θ θ θ

And of course why must I never write, if not because this is what I would write? This, my life, which was never meant to be a seed but merely the fruit of another's.

θ θ θ

("   all
    This   happened,"
                            .)

θ θ θ

In seventh grade, one morning just like every other morning, I waited for the bus, sitting on the stone wall welded together with graying concrete and scrubby lichen, reading and oblivious to the sweet spring gloam of moist light and the early conversations of birds in the trees. I usually got to the stop a half hour early, consequence of my (my mother's) anxious fear that I might be late, so a book passed the time and kept me from having to think of existing in the world.

This morning, though, down the street at the next corner was a group of other kids my age. Public-school kids, since I didn't know any of them. Where had they come from? Before this day it was always just me, alone with my stone wall and my book. Whatever schedule or bus route change had realigned these tandem worlds into one, it made me very uncomfortable. While they waited they played a quick game of kickball in the street. One of them came over and asked me if I wanted to join them. "No, thanks," I mumbled, and he just stood there for a bit, a little confused, I think, then turned around and walked back to the game.

It was just that one day. Whatever moves conjured this conjunction slipped away, and tandem worlds returned to their separate courses, leaving me alone again, anxiously happy with my stone wall and my book and the morning light that I was completely oblivious to.

θ θ θ

During the evenings alone with my mother asleep on the couch by seven after her twelve-hour work shift, fingers green or blue from the dyes she handled all day at the chemical plant, I would watch her sleep and her face soften and wonder if corpses were this way. I hated her for trapping me in the intimacy of this voyeurism that more properly belonged to a lover than a son, and I feared that one breath would fall out of her slack mouth and not climb back in but flutter like invisible seeds into me. My inheritance: this bitterness, this exhaustion.

θ θ θ

During the school year it was my mind that was expansive: coursing cascades of long division, scrutinizing the fine-toothed roads of grade-school theology, making the rut of the ordered procession of bells and chalkboard eraser claps, monthly school masses, and afternoon bus rides into a polished groove to conduct this hollowed half-life. The last day of school was always bewildering and melancholy for just this reason: Without the rut, where is the road? Without the road, where is the future? Without the future, where is the will to seed?

θ θ θ

Shepherd's purse leaves in summer, pinnatifid like barnacle tongues or serrated for cutting away all delusion, are bitter and acrid as they contain more of the stimulating principle racing to seed. In the summer the rest of the world closes in, mountains of water rise from level ground and valley what was once wide.

θ θ θ

The summer rose up, closed me up in a humid coffin. During the days alone while she was at work (seniority finally meaning she worked first shift), I would lie naked on the bed with the large mirror over the dresser at its foot and roll on my back until my legs catapulted over my hips and around my ears, my ass in the air, my balls in the damp heat sloshing down, and my erect cock trembling against the thick plume of hair that had already been with me for a few years already, though I was only twelve. This reversal of gravity and the rhythmic breeze of the ceiling fan made my asshole gawp open and a sudden coolness whisper against it. Open, I was trapped, young already growing bitter, rushing to seed.

θ θ θ

(" all
This happened,"
.)

θ θ θ

Eighth grade: another year, another bus stop, another daily con-
tention with my moment-to-moment desire to disappear while
standing in the cold of a New England winter morning on an
exposed sidewalk corner. This time on busy Main Street, across
from where I lived and in front of a group residence for troubled
teens. No place to sit and too busy with passing cars to will
myself into being the only person in the world, I had to brave the
cold and look at the sidewalk.

"Hey faggot! What are you doing down there?"

I turned around to see this sixteen- or seventeen-year-old guy
leaning out his open window, bare-chested in the winter cold.
His arms were creamy white and hairless. His pecs were big
enough to cast shadows on his stomach and were also hairless,
spotted only by two dark-brown nipples. His tousled dark hair
and his slurred snarl and his crooked teeth scared me a little, as if
he were going to climb right out of the second-floor window and
come at me like an angry dog. Instead we stared at each other for
a second or two and then he closed his window. I turned back
around to face the street and acted as if nothing had happened,
resolved now to try harder to be the only person in the world.

For years I would remember that bare chest, those heavy pecs,
that mess of hair and teeth, and fantasize about him letting me
in through the front door and up to his bedroom. For years I
would imagine what could have happened if I had spoken.

θ θ θ

"I will never have grandchildren."

Actually, though I had endlessly imagined what this day would be like, this was one response I had never considered. It was so baffling, so decentering because it was not about me at all.

I was sixteen, and though it would be another two years and a world away in New York that I would first kiss a man, I had returned home from high school one day to find my mother weeping. Having thought it appropriate to read my journal, she had learned that day what I had come to terms with a year earlier—that I was gay. When she sat me down in our living room, this was all she could say through a storm of tears.

Staring emotionless through the window at the empty blue sky, I finally managed to respond.

"You can either make this easier or harder for me. You get to choose."

And she did.

θ θ θ

("   all
This   happened,"
                              .)

3: Pilgrim-Weed

θ θ θ

St. James, pilgrim-pastor, martyred in the East, cradled in a floating mountain arked by angels across the sea, set down in the West at the end of the world: pray for me, pay for me this heavy toll.

θ θ θ

Stone boat, riding the course of stars all the way to the end, is there room for one more? At the wheel, in the crow's nest, at an oar, in the hold, keel-clutching, anchor-weight spinning in the heavy press of darkness?

If you know where you'll land, then I'm going.

If you don't know where you're headed, then I'm going.

θ θ θ

Pilgrimage: Meeting Point: Lost in the pulsating dark.

One night, fourteen years old and alone while my mother took the always-accepted overtime and toiled under the sodium-light-lit smokestacks of the chemical factory where she processed paint dyes, I slipped out of the house, restless. I waited for her nightly phone call from work, the one that made sure no catastrophe had snatched me while the necessities of life took her away from guarding me. Then, half afraid that stepping past my front door alone might indeed kill me, I walked out into the cool night air, front door locked and double-checked, unlocked and relocked to make sure my key worked, keys dropped into my pocket and then felt for in a panic to make sure they were still there.

I walked through empty neighborhood streets, my own neighborhood, but down streets I had never seen, across a map of a near-world I had never known in daylight, let alone darkness. I skipped around the edges of the streetlight orbits so as to be unseen. I walked briskly with an urgency of false confidence, as if someone at any moment might question my presence and snuff me out. I was going nowhere and everywhere, having never gone before.

At the bottom of a hill was a culvert and a small path into a woodlot dense and thicketed among the houses of this development. I turned right onto the path, and the moon made every one of last year's dead leaves glow white, every one of this year's living leaves glow blue.

I am a bowl of water, gleaming in the moonlight, gleaming in the dark, unseen by any eye.

What drew me in was the high-pitched tinkling of a million bells in waving wind, first one gust and then another, camps of bells on the end of each branch calling out to each other—these spring frogs, whose voices swarmed and shimmered around this bowl of silver water, water slivered by sound into a million shivering moons.

Small pool of water, precipice of sound, the wind catches and the seeds blow.

θ θ θ

Pilgrimage: End of the World: New York City, 1994.

The answer could only be to leave. Swept away on a scholarship to NYU, seedy and anxious to germinate, I left as best I could, which is to say with as little of my life as possible. But still, food in boxes obsessively wrapped in packing tape covering every surface arrived in the mail. She made eight-hour round trips from Rhode Island to New York and back, just so she could spend four hours of awkwardness, wandering a city she hated with a son who didn't want her there. And always the bags and bags of groceries, these furiously hurled seeds of the need to be needed.

θ θ θ

What interior twisted strand of history passes unseen through one body to another, running across an autumn field of time, running from itself, endlessly?

θ θ θ

Green-curl: bitter—unthunk, unseen, for you're everywhere.
White-whirl: crucifer—stipple stitch in raceme running you.

Heart-seed: who holds you when I let go into the wind?
Life-wand: incant the word I'm waiting for, spring me.

θ θ θ

Where did the wind misdirect the pollen to? When did the seed uncurl into this? What was so unwanted, extra excess excrescence of love? Why weed the meadow of cress? Why we'd meadow the lawn of course, if we had our way. Who reaped this weedy harvest, hay in the loft humming with seed, a dangerous damp fire of love? How to put out, once started, this catastrophe of love?

θ θ θ

In my heart there is a seed. In my seed there is a heart, spilled without care:

Remember his maroon-plaid, banded-collar shirt and tight jeans, his squinting broad smile, his strumming guitar and Indigo Girls serenade, sitting in a stairwell until a rainy November dawn over East Tenth Street.

Remember the kiss, and his fingers playing Chopin on my ribs as we fell asleep.

Remember the unexpected appearance at the front door . . . the hands held while Texas sunlight poured like honey across the movie screen . . . boundaries breaking . . . seed-soaked in an orchard at night . . . bucking thighs in a dorm room . . . hoisted up against a wall and eased down, one door down from his sleeping mother.

Remember the foolish grin in the dappled light on the bench under the willow tree and the sheepish clear eyes around each turn on the garden-parade circuit. Remember the stroll along Clinton Street under pear blossoms and the climb up the Rivington Street stairs to his hermit's apartment with birdcages hung like twigged labyrinths from the ceiling. Remember the breeze on the fire escape.

Remember the embrace of soft flannel, the fresh smell of sand and sea at the nape of his neck, the sweetness.

Remember the flutter of cream in a room full of still black, the kohled eyes and philosophizing on tree stumps. Remember the small town stroll, the shoulders bumping, sliding, resting against each other. Remember the graveyard and the soft grass and the lying there hinged and the decision to lean over.

Remember the gray-green sip, the kiss, the hinge-swing opening as his arms closed around me.

θ θ θ

("   all

This   happened,"

                                         .)

θ θ θ

Pilgrimage: Meeting Point: Apocrypha.

Lounging in the long blades of grass, far from the world, one shepherd buries his face into the stubbled neck of the other, alternately kissing, biting, and giggling as the other's hands search under clothes, through tangles of hair. The night is mild and the air between them is heavy; the stars are the only eyes looking down on them and they are far far away. No need for the cover of a blanket out here. The sheep are scattered across the hills in bleating clumps, completely ignored.

When the sky lightens with the flaming of a great star and wheels of singing fire turn in concentric gyres from horizon to horizon they stop for a moment, then the one climbs on top of the other, presses his weight against him, blots out the sky with the cloud of his black curls, and fills the other's mouth with the speech of his own tongue.

θ θ θ

Pilgrimage: Underworld: East Twelfth Street and Third Avenue, 1996.

Flinty seed at the center of a dry papery heart.

The first time I went to the theater with no marquee and passed through the glass doors covered over with reflective mylar, soft ridges of corduroy pressed against the turnstile bar at the counter in dim fluorescent light, and I pushed my way through with my crotch. Seated in the back, I waited to be carried away by the grunting flicker of electric shadows on the screen or by the smooth white face that slid into the seat two away from me only a few minutes after I arrived.

After one moment and then one more, the face slid closer, into the seat next to mine. I was in a foreign land and there was the awkwardness and the thrill of not being able to communicate. Hand signals would have to suffice. The face grew hands and they reached past the waistband of his sweatpants to pull out a cock, pale and white. They cradled it as the face stared right into my eyes. I looked from cock to screen to eyes to cock to screen to corduroy lap. Learning the language of this place, my own hands gestured nervously in reciprocal greeting, tugging in jerks at the zipper, begging the button out of its hole. After a while he leaned over and his heavy breath asked, "What are you doing here? You're too young for this. This is a place for old men."

θ θ θ

The vault of heaven is surmised to be three fingers thick. If I reach for a star, pinprick, sphincter of God and with first one finger then two then three—

—then I could escape this need to generate
—then fold this flock inside me into eternity
—then calm my karma, plant no-seed in no-one
—then leave my roots behind, catapult ultraviolet
—then contrail petal-radiant past pollination past past

θ θ θ

Pilgrimage: End of the World: Flickerville Mountain Farm, Warfordsburg, PA, 1998.

No place farther from New York City and Rhode Island, these fifteen acres of organic farmland, this sore back and these blistered then calloused fingers, these Milky Way nights and thunderhead afternoons at the lake across the road. After a life trapped in the coffin of my head trapped in the claustrophobic hole-in-the-ground of my family, at twenty-one I struck out, climbed a ladder leaned against the limits and stuck my hands through to the other side, deep in rotting ground and lacquered green-black after picking thousands of tomatoes.

Despite my best efforts and explicit demands to be left alone, she followed me. Manic, pretending not to be exhausted from driving twelve hours straight from Rhode Island into these backwoods of Pennsylvania, she arrived—and refused to step any farther than the driveway, repelled completely and utterly by the reality of her son working here on this farm, this farm she spent a lifetime escaping, across oceans, across universes.

θ θ θ

Pilgrimage: Meeting Point: Lost in dappled light.

Done with a day of work at the farm, I walked down the hill and through the curtain of marginal brambles and shrubs into the woods, dense with quiet. Finding a level spot, I stripped my clothes off, sat cross-legged on the dry leaves and cotton-like duff, and closed my eyes.

I am a bowl of smoke, empty and calmly revolving.

When I opened my eyes, four deer stood three feet from me. I felt on my back, my lap, my upturned soles, the warmth of the spots of light that settled on their backs. We looked at each other for a long time.

θ θ θ

Pilgrimage: End of the World: Soca, 1998.

Stupidly, I took her up on her offer to go to Uruguay. Me: dread-locked yogi-farmer. Her: recently self-excised from all her family and friends by an argument in which she packed up all her history with them—friendship, mutual aid, and resentments—and resolved to be alone (well, almost. She always had her son).

Once there, we stayed as we always did at my Tía Martha's house. In Soca, nothing much happens except sitting under the grape arbor on Tía's patio, reading. At most, under a noonday blaze of sun I might walk from one end of the small town to the other to visit with my tías Olga and Miriam at their houses.

No one knew what to do with this man in dreadlocks, like an alien on their doorstep. Everyone was polite. No one was enthusiastic.

"I told Tía Martha," she said timidly and resignedly one morning, finding me out on the patio.

"Sorry? You told her what?" I asked, confused.

"I told her about you being . . . gay," she whispered, as if someone might overhear her English in this small Uruguayan town and understand her.

I was so angry at her presumption that I could have gotten up right then and walked down the road, out of the town, and all the way to the airport. I should have. I didn't.

θ θ θ

Pilgrimage: End of the World: St. Mark's Bookshop, 1999.

At twenty-one I was depressed and a complete failure. My four years in college had yielded nothing but regret and a sense of incompetence. My season of farming had been cut short by the intrusions of a mother desperate for access to her son and a disastrous trip to Uruguay.

I returned to New York tentatively, thanks to the generosity of the one with the birdcages strung up on the ceiling of his little Lower East Side studio apartment. We were two gentle fools in the world, easily hurt and easily sent into our shells. Lucky for me he shared his little shell, and we were like the Han Shan and Shi De of Rivington Street. The best this scholarship kid graduated from NYU magna cum laude could manage was a clerk job at St. Mark's Bookshop. It was a place to be, among books and among kindred spirits: an oasis.

It was also a place where I hid—in the bathroom or downstairs in the stockroom or in the mystery section—from former professors when they came in lest I have to explain myself to them. It was a time of hiding from shortfalls and making small progress toward capability in the world by shelving books and getting paid for it.

θ θ θ

Pilgrimage: Asymptote.

Lost but determined to find a compass, map, or blaze, once a week I made the forty-five-minute walk from the Lower East Side to the far West Village to see a therapist. I entered through the brownstone's front gate and then door, through the always completely empty and clean kitchen and living room, up the narrow staircase and into the cedar-paneled room where the overstuffed tan leather chair awaited me. She sat down in its counterpart opposite. Light from the window filtered in onto us and the large painting of a small crying schoolboy in shadows that hung between us.

I was there because I couldn't take it anymore, this uselessness and this sadness that each week seemed to find its predictable origin in my mother. Every week my therapist tried another way to get me to say it, and every week I found another story to tell to avoid it.

"Why can't you be angry?"

θ θ θ

Pilgrimage: Heredity.

If I had solved the equation my therapist laid out before me each week, I would have left and never come back. To own up to this anger would have meant disappearing into the infinite world.

Like my father before me.

θ θ θ

Pilgrimage: Function.

But a function is always two, tethered to each other, and the trick of this life I've never gotten free of is this hopeless desire to simply be functional, ironed into me by my mother's relentless refrain when I was a child:

"No seas inútil." (Don't be useless.)

Except of course as the other half of the shape of life.

θ θ θ

Pilgrimage: Meeting Point: Zendo, New York City.

How many times does a door need to be walked past before it is opened?

The planted seed: how long before it brunts its head up into the light? There is frustration, temptation, boredom, and anger, but nothing happens.

Sitting in the dark, one thing becomes another, seamlessly, and nothing has happened.

Facing a blank white wall on a square of black.

The heel of one foot touches down alongside the arch of the other.

Every body in the room curls into itself together, this blooming of seeds returning to their dark ground.

Finally the freedom of   being, not being   seen.

θ θ θ

Pilgrimage: End of the World: Three Sheep, Camino de Santiago, 2000.

The old man walked with his flock, an endless stream of bucking sheep crossing the highway until they overtook me and my walking companions and we all moved together. In one hand a walking stick, in the other a newborn lamb swinging from its held hind legs, across his shoulders a second one, four legs dangling across his chest and the soft warm belly along the creases of his neck's weathered nape.

Walking alone along a narrow path, I saw a pile of muddy rubbish up ahead. Not until I got about ten feet away did I realize that this mess was a sheep calmly lying on its back, its legs buckled up limp in the air. It did nothing as I approached but look at me dumbly. Its wool was matted with mud in great plates. How long had it been here, immobile and paralyzed by futility or stupidity or both? Without thinking I reached deep into the crusted wool, grabbed two handfuls, and lifted its deadweight up. Almost before the feet hit the ground, it bounded away with ferocious speed, but for a moment I held the mud-caked universe in my hands.

I was descending the rocky slope into the valley in failing autumn twilight when from over the next ridge an unseen shepherd's rough voice began swearing the foulest curses at his invisible flock. The torrent of abuse continued without stopping for at least fifteen minutes, until some shifting parallax of our changing locations cut it off from my ears. All that was left were the dried grasses of the end of the year on the facing ridge, shining ghosts in the light, waving with the passing breeze.

θ θ θ

Pilgrimage: End of the World: Cruz de Hierro, Camino de Santiago, 2000.

Past the nearly abandoned village of Manjarín—just stacks of stones, dirty geese wandering in the fog, the hospitality of a lunatic with his vinegary fish stew and noxious leaky stovepipe—at the highest point of the mountain pass lay the Cruz de Hierro, the Iron Cross, a telephone pole planted in stone, telegraphing holy messages up into the sky through its tiny mounted iron cross. When I came to place my call it was November and the fog obliterated everything beyond the reach of my outstretched hand as I followed the cindery path of shattered slate through rough gorse.

Here at this end of the world, hundreds of thousands of stones were piled around the flanks of the cross, a hill some twenty or thirty feet in diameter and six or seven feet high. Carried by pilgrims from their front doorsteps, the weight and shape of their sins, the load of their history passed like chromosomes, each stone was a seed cast over the shoulder of the traveler at the cross. Lord, deliver me from my evil! Let this seed not grow but let it lie here forever at this meeting of land and sky. Let my karma die here or climb up this ladder to the stars and pass through and out, forever.

Here, these end-of-worlders like me: blown into the corners.

θ θ θ

Pilgrimage: Meeting Point: Moss, 2002.

Looking for a love of something that might anchor me in place, I looked again to plants, training as a horticulturist at the Brooklyn Botanic Garden. Like book shelving before, a simple routine was all I could hope for and handle.

On the shaded concrete steps leading up to the Overlook Terrace, on the bare soil on the edges of the artificial stream running through the garden's center, in the cracks between the bricks where the sun pounded down in Magnolia Plaza, I found moss. The smallest of the smallest plants in fifty-two acres of garden in the middle of Brooklyn.

Moss: without roots, so the leaves that absorb water directly huddle tight together to trap droplets with surface tension; without veins and vessels, so the skin is so thin it lets everything in, a plant of nothing but skin; without defense, so every single cell ripped away is its defense against extinction, able to fully reclaim life from death by rebuilding itself anew.

Totipotent.

θ θ θ

Pilgrimage: End of the World: Thought Experiments in Horticulture, 2002.

Two hedgerows and a narrow lawn stretched between. A green walkway between gray-brown walls in early spring. At one end a red-twigged dogwood—bare bones on fire, flame against fog. The dogwood suckers forth a foot, two feet, in front. Behind: the past scythed down, a foot, two feet. Memory harvested, wattled and daubed, hidden into history's walls or casually thrown out on a brush pile. Twenty-six years later and two hedgerows with a narrow lawn between, a red-twigged dogwood stands how far down to the other end? Is it the same? Has anything changed?

And the shepherd's purse? Lost and rooted in the lawn, until one day without expectation or consciousness, it explodes in flower and seed and wind and meadows the lawn, flies through the hedgerows, sails on light to the very end of the world and past.

θ θ θ

Pilgrimage: End of the World Meeting Point: Anywhere but here.

My life has been delineated by great-circle arcs of travel. Paris, Pyrenees, Istanbul.

Each a new life proposed, a piece of me cast into possibility. Hong Kong, Lisbon, Kerala.

If circumstance conspired, would I have refused? Pilgrimage, houseboat, forest walk.

Where the vault of heaven bows down to meet the earthly plane or swirling sea there is a meeting point. At the end of the world: meniscus.

An urge to climb, these stacks of ladders.

θ θ θ

On the road of an uncertain pilgrimage, when the end is shift-ing, how to calculate one's beginnings? Lingering by the sunset window of a borrowed home in Rhode Island, curled inside a fist pushing embers across linens in Uruguay, candled in the belly of a boat, whistled from Lanzarote dragon tree to dragon tree, or even further back.

There are moments of transport, movement strung on a thread of paralysis:

a bicycle and a boy, unseen, flying

a night walk and a wall of sound, greeting the ghost of the
universe

a white wall and a half hour of breath, circling the circus of the
mind

θ θ θ

Pilgrimage: End of the World: El Chaltén, Patagonia, 2008.

Far past my heart-shaped land of Uruguay, across the muddy waters of the Río de la Plata, twenty hours out of Buenos Aires through endless blazes of sunflower fields that nevertheless ended, over the stony bones of Neuquén dinosaurs locked in pink moonscape hills, along the shore of the crystal lake at Bariloche while waiting for a bus connection, down the sloping mountain-pass highways where twenty years before only packhorses could pick their way to El Bolsón, into a permaculture paradise one kilometer hiked in off the dirt road to its mud dancing and its swimming hole icy cold, out back to the world past acres of hopvines twining up guidelines, forward, twenty-four hours forward on Ruta 40, ripio-reverberated guanaco-hearted leaping and dancing in the wind and the emptiness of the steppe until at three in the morning I arrived at the almost-end, El Chaltén, a pinprick of a town at the entrance to a kingdom of rock and ice and water at the bottom of the world.

θ θ θ

One light: myriad colors. One tree: forever forests. One water: silver cloud, turquoise ice, milk-white torrent.

For three days I climbed through Nothofagus forests, their small, leathery leaves and contorted limbs, one species cloaking the lower flanks of the mountains in shade; up bare scree, the broken remnants of titanic clashes of air and water and earth; under brilliant ultraviolet sunshine pouring down unseen; across churning rivers silver with suspended minerals, the one-railed branch bridge bouncing with each step; below low clouds ferrying water softly in drops, mists, flakes of snow to the source.

θ θ θ

On the morning of the third day I woke up.

θ θ θ

I climbed the dawn-lit cirque of rubble and saw the glacier,

θ θ θ

father of all, its hundred-foot-high façade crumbling

θ θ θ

seeding the turquoise lake at its feet

θ θ θ

with the future.

θ θ θ

```
                    θ
                  θ   θ
                θ   θ   θ
              θ   θ   θ   θ
            θ   θ   θ   θ   θ
          θ   θ   θ   θ   θ   θ
        θ   θ   θ   θ   θ   θ   θ
      θ   θ   θ   θ   θ   θ   θ   θ
    θ   θ   θ   θ   θ   θ   θ   θ   θ
  θ   θ   θ   θ   θ   θ   θ   θ   θ   θ
θ   θ   θ   θ   θ   θ   θ   θ   θ   θ   θ
θ   θ   θ   θ   θ   θ   θ   θ   θ   θ   θ   θ
θ   θ   θ   θ   θ   θ   θ   θ   θ   θ   θ   θ   θ
θ   θ   θ   θ   θ   θ   θ   θ   θ   θ   θ   θ   θ   θ
θ   θ   θ   θ   θ   θ   θ   θ   θ   θ   θ   θ   θ   θ   θ
θ   θ   θ   θ   θ   θ   θ   θ   θ   θ   θ   θ   θ   θ   θ   θ
θ   θ   θ   θ   θ   θ   θ   θ   θ   θ   θ   θ   θ   θ   θ   θ   θ
θ   θ   θ   θ   θ   θ   θ   θ   θ   θ   θ   θ   θ   θ   θ   θ   θ   θ
θ   θ   θ   θ   θ   θ   θ   θ   θ   θ   θ   θ   θ   θ   θ   θ   θ   θ   θ
θ   θ   θ   θ   θ   θ   θ   θ   θ   θ   θ   θ   θ   θ   θ   θ   θ   θ   θ   θ
θ   θ   θ   θ   θ   θ   θ   θ   θ   θ   θ   θ   θ   θ   θ   θ   θ   θ   θ   θ   θ
θ   θ   θ   θ   θ   θ   θ   θ   θ   θ   θ   θ   θ   θ   θ   θ   θ   θ   θ   θ   θ   θ
```

[Fathers, Figured]

"He hides inside his forgetfulness
The other looks for him in the grass"

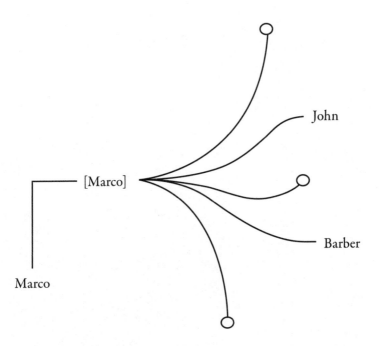

[Substitutions 1:
A House of Swinging Doors:
This Future Life
(*Calvatia gigantea*)]

What leaf? What mushroom?
—BASHŌ (TRANSLATED BY JOHN CAGE)

Amid the September leaf litter bronzed by the slanting afternoon light, a gleaming skull, round and clean, catches my eye. First one, then another further off the trail, and another smaller one like a child's, and over there is a white knob like a hip joint unsocketed and emerging from the ground.

"Botanizers are the worst out here. You've got to unscrew those green eyes from their sockets and put them away. No more flowers or leaf shapes," advises John, my forest guide for this mushroom foraging class. We soft-step through the leaf litter, scrutinizing every shadow, every tree stump and rotting log, every clump of leaves tilted up as if by some tiny earthquake. "You've got to screw in your brown eyes and look for shades of brown and red, violet and orange, caps and shelves and spheres."

I'm not sure what to do with the stark white hairs that have been showing up in my beard the past few years or how to reconcile feeling still so young and so unprepared for the world with these pigmentless ghosts already congregating on my chin. My hair is dark brown and thick like the hair of my never-known father, whose head bore heavy waves of black in a blurred 1970s photograph, the only one I have ever seen of him (and that one not since I was seven years old). Through my beard runs a sheen of copper, inheritance from my mother, of her rich auburn hair that used to fall in a long, straight cascade down her back when I was a child. Now her hair is thin and cropped short to her head, a cap of snow curled around her skull. Occasionally I pull at the white in my beard, my eyes crossing as I try to measure depth in the bathroom mirror, either with my fingers or with tweezers, not so much out of vanity as out of grotesque curiosity at the feel of the oddly thick, coarse hairs as I spin them between thumb and index finger.

John and I are searching for mushrooms—like Virgil leading Dante through the dark woods and into the underworld—out of the green and gold of leaves spinning sugar from air and down into the forest duff, the mulch and mildew of moisture caught and webbed into the ground. Through the dark-brown soil run thick, waxy-white threads, individuals that merge into cords, cords that merge into mats, mats that grab hold of last year's fallen leaves, chew them into humus, and mold them into tilth. These mycelia are a headless, toothless, limbless, eyeless body. A body of all nerves or all blood vessels, a network-body, a net, a mind.

One cell inhabits a space, its membrane a provisional line of limit, though in reality the quantity and variety of transactions across that line make of the cell a house built of nothing but swinging doors. When one cell becomes two cells becomes four cells becomes eight, there might be infinite city blocks or there might be one swirling liquid dragon endlessly jumping through hoops of flame.

The mycelial mat of a fungus under the veneer of leaves in a forest is like the internet, according to the mycologist Paul Stamets. It pulses with information that is at once everywhere and nowhere. Headless, it thinks. Toothless, it eats. Sexless, it mounts its desire into the ether of air in fantastic architectures of gills and caps and pores.

Birth: two cells find each other: two turning into one, two turning into a third, turning turning some notion of self into a scaffold for community, community conjuring dreams of webs, congeries of roots and ganglia: a body.

There are some thirty-seven trillion cells in my body. Some are human and others are bacteria, viruses, fungi. Only one of ten is mine, begging the question, "Am I theirs?"

For most of my life my mother has been overprotective and possessive of me, covetous of my attention and affection whenever it's been given elsewhere. Now, in her seventies and slowed by Parkinson's disease, she has come to stay with my partner and me in our house. I cut slabs of olive bread and slices of salty salami for lunch with her on my back porch on a summer afternoon. I watch her when she walks to make sure she doesn't trip. I observe her in a thousand small moments to make sure she is O.K. Her thinning white hairs entangle with my coarsening white hairs. A door swings one way and then another, and a spirit flies past.

In the forest, fungi comprise 40 percent of all the life in the soil, and mycorrhizal fungi form symbiotic relationships with some 90 percent of all plants on the planet. Plants, it turns out, are for the most part quite ill-equipped to absorb the nutrients necessary for life on their own. Fungi, on the other hand, are ravenous. With powerful enzymes that can break down intractable substances like the lignin that makes wood woody, fungi are excellent nutrient absorbers. So good that the livers of several hapless mycophiles are liquefied every year by an unwisely eaten destroying angel. On one of our forays, John laughs, "There are old mushroom hunters, and there are bold mushroom hunters, but there are no old, bold mushroom hunters." While plants catch sunlight and bounce it through narrow, green-glowing channels of chloroplasts in leaves high in the air, fungi tunnel underground, melting away this illusion of a solid world into wisps and fragments. Fungi send molecules across vast waxy-white networks of mycelia to plants, and plants reciprocate with sugars sent down stems and trunks to roots, which fungal hairs clasp and even penetrate.

More than just a symbiotic relationship, the interface of plant and fungus is a medium of communication. A tree in a forest speaks to its sisters in chemical words written on the white scroll of mycelia unfurling underground. One tree may nourish another by sending nutrients that are shuttled by fungus connecting to both. The door swings and energy flows.

John shows me black trumpets, soft and velvety with an olive tint, and almost immediately I start seeing them everywhere.

We come upon a peppery bolete, with its massive twelve-inch tawny cap standing six inches off the ground on a sturdy stem, and he casually breaks off a hunk of cap to show the pleasing yellow flesh inside. "Touch it to your tongue," he says, offering the chunk my way. I look skeptical, but he is insistent, so I do and recoil instantly at the immediate and overwhelming acrid bitterness. "That'll teach you," he chuckles. And then in the distance, he points at the gleaming white dome, some eighteen inches across and rising out of the leaves. This is the giant puffball, *Calvatia gigantea*. John palms it underneath and, with a firm tug and an audible snap, lifts it up. He flicks his index finger against it and it gives a satisfyingly rich thump, like the stretched skin of a drum. He passes it to me, and it must easily be ten pounds, a medicine ball of a mushroom. Inside it is pure white and the consistency of firm marshmallow.

Calvatia gigantea: the giant skull. At first it is a spot of milk on the ground, then a golf ball, then a baby's soft skull, delicate and still knitting together. It grows over several days, monstrously. The skull's skin hardens into a dull matte, healing over the adolescent ruptures of too-quick growth. Grown to its full majesty, immediately it descends into decay. The fine-textured white interior coarsens, sickens into a dingy ocher chartreuse, as its trillions of spores mature. The skin thins and brittles. The wind, weight, or an animal inevitably snaps the neck of this teetering skull and the contents tumble out, a graceful exhalation of ocher smoke into the quiet of the autumn forest.

Calvo: "bald" in Spanish. To be bald is to be one step closer to one's skull. Gleaming taut skin across hard bone. I think about my maternal uncles, most of whom are bald, as was my mother's father. And on my father's side I have no idea if I even have uncles.

Only smoke. Dead: the baldest one can be, when even skin and blood are shed away and only unyielding bone remains.

John, though I only knew him briefly, was a kind of father, a filament passing through me into smoke. He died of a heart attack two years after our foraging expedition. Not the heroic/tragic/ironic death by an ill-identified mushroom in one last fatal meal, but of a prosaic heart attack, the result of a plaquey artery or a misfiring muscle. He was too young to have died, but he was a large man who, though surprisingly nimble in the trailless forest, was an imposing ponderous figure short of breath as he bent over tiny caps poking out from under dry dead leaves.

While some fungi are pathogenic and predatory, many others are saprophytic, feasting only on the dead. How do they know a corpse from a life? What are the limits and contours of a fungus's knowing? I myself wonder at and worry the edge of life, trembling in unforeseeable secret moments at the prospect of my own end. As a child I watched my mother asleep on the couch by eight p.m. after working for twelve hours in a factory, and I feared the moment when her caving-in chest wouldn't rise back up. What then? And now, in the middle of my life that was always only ever meant to be a substitute for a hole in hers, I listen to her labored breathing in the close of her life and wonder. When one day the labor ends, in the moment after that moment, what then?

The ancient Greeks believed mushrooms to be the fruit of lightning strikes, from their observation that after a night of fierce storms the woods and meadows would suddenly be covered in fungus of all manner of strange colors and shapes. Such bizarre "plants" that appear from nowhere could only come from something equally powerful and mysterious, like bolts of divine fire. Without mouths or orifices of any kind, fungal hyphae exude powerful enzymes into the soil around them. They do the work of breaking material down into soluble component molecules that are then absorbed into the cells. Like an external stomach (though not like this at all), these enzymes form an aura of dissolution around the fungus, a liminal zone of other transforming into self, of self extending past itself in a halo of becoming. Do fungi have selves? Humans, of course, are more horrifying, given that we eat the living and keep our stomachs inside us like black holes of light that trap and transform the spirits of living things into ourselves.

When I die I want (though I will be past wanting) to be buried without a casket or shroud, naked, completely unadorned, and have a fruit tree planted above me (above that which is not me), so that its roots might plunge hungry into (not) my stomach, curious into (not) my brain, desirous into (not) my pelvis, thirsty into (not) my mouth.

In a presentation on her proposal for fungus funeral suits, Jae Rhim Lee describes a suit or shroud to be wrapped around the deceased. The suit is inoculated with fungi that will decompose the body, cocooning it in a nest of white threads, impelling it toward transformation. The impetus for this project is to neutralize all the toxins (heavy metals in particular) that accumulate in the modern industrialized human body (cyborg at the level of mercury and lead and strontium enmeshed in kidneys, liver, and marrow). Call this atonement for a collective careless life, a life without care that has collected in lazy cellular eddies the contaminants of a lifetime. Call this absolution: dispersal of a life's sins in hyphal tides, enzymatic ripples. To expedite this process, Lee suggests cultivating the agent of your posthumous expiation by feeding a culture of fungus your toe-nail clippings and dead skin, breeding over your own lifetime a strain of fungus uniquely attuned to undo you.

In old apple orchards, white and pink flowers cloud the sky in branches unpruned and entangled with each other. At their gnarled feet in the unmown grass, morels fruit from the rich dark earth. In my black sleep, in my white dreams, a single prayer: a swinging door.

"My father knew a lot about these things," my mother says. (What does my own father know? And what does he know of what his father knew? Lost threads rising to smoke.) She tells me, after asking me if I have any ashes to coat the seed potatoes we are about to plant in the ground, that he used to do this all the time. She remembers this from her childhood, as well as how he used tobacco to ward off insects from potato plants. Fine threads of memory unspool from her white skull under-neath her cap of white hair. Each day another white hair appears in my beard.

Under a microscope's shifting focus, cells can appear like indi-vidual walled medieval cities, buzzing with activity contained by heavily fortified borders. Or with the turn of a knob, the walls all fall and leave a unified maze of interconnecting alley-ways, a shimmering lace of movement, an open field. On a late autumn day as golden light slants in across the dry grass, who can say where one begins and another ends? Who would want to? With each breeze, doors swing. Light roots the ground. Grass stitches the sky.

It's been many years now since John passed away. His brown eyes have long gone white in the soil. What do they see now? Perhaps they squint at the sun, green-gold now in the leaves at the very top of a hundred-foot oak. Or maybe they sift, transparent in the millions, from velvety gills into the forest air. In my sleep, maybe they rolled out of the earth, unspooling white threads from their last home, crossed highways and valleys, and nuzzled their way past my eyelids into my sockets, so that now a waxy white cord runs from John to me, conducting like electricity a memory of a way of seeing. Two nodes of a network, one spirit flying from door to door.

There are some woods a half hour west of my house where I go on pilgrimage. Each year sometime around Labor Day, I make my way there and walk a trail that crosses a river and switchbacks up a hill, goes through a stand of pines and the soft susurrus of dry needles underfoot, and finally comes to a spot that is completely unremarkable. Off the path (now a gravel road) to the right and down a slight shady incline among a thick leaf litter, I always find without fail the relics of this quest, these holy bones. Skulls, hip joints, knobs of tibia: a heap, a string, a constellation: the visible part of something so much larger and unseen: *Calvatia gigantea*.

My mother wants to be cremated when she dies. It's actually been a while since she's mentioned this, though she used to remind me all the time when I was a child of eight or nine—over dinner, while walking through the aisles of a toy store, driving me to school in the morning. "I don't want to be buried underground. Remember, I want to be cremated and then spread my ashes at the ocean." This was information I hardly knew what to do with at that age. Less a question of fear, my unease in these moments had more to do with some sense of the morbid inappropriateness of speaking of this, as if such speech came through a portal out of some other world. Now, with my mother in her seventies, I think I can appreciate more the radical gesture of cremation, this act that so forcefully impresses on its survivors the transformation of the deceased. The fire of burial, on the other hand, is an exceedingly slow burn. It is the work of a trillion small enzymatic bonfires in each fungal thread turning flesh into soil.

I palm a puffball, small as a newborn's skull and as soft, with my index and middle fingers on either side of the delicate little vertebral cord connecting it to its gargantuan body beneath, and with a light pressure snap it. Others are much larger: grapefruits, soccer balls, basketballs. One looks like an albino piglet curled up asleep, another is two feet across and must weigh ten pounds or more. When I get home I find that one of the larger ones is already too far gone, all golden and curdled inside. I tear it into large hunks as if ripping apart a giant loaf of bread and scatter them about the yard. Over the next year, as I pass them I will give them gentle nudges with my foot or pick them up and squeeze them like playing a bandoneón. Ocher smoke billows out, even a year later, like curls off a trillion pyres. Smoke, spores, this swinging door, this future life.

[Substitutions 2: Among Men]

The cracked red leather of the barber's chair creaks and its rusted gears whine as I settle in, ready in this sweat-slicked heat of Kerala in February to be rid of the beard that has been with me all through my Ohio autumn and winter. I have catapulted seasons across the world from my home by ice-locked Lake Erie to the burning winter fog of Delhi and the icy nights of Dehradun and Mussoorie in the north, and now finally south to Kochi, Indian city and hundred-degree cauldron boiling next to the Arabian Sea. Three days in, and my facial hair has become intolerable. My savior is a small man in his sixties standing in front of his barbershop. His head bears just the silvered tonsure of age and a clean, gleaming dome, and his own face is grizzled with whiskers. Who barbers the barber, here at the Shalimar Saloon?

After he drapes a deep red cloth across me, out come the electric clippers and a few breezy sweeps later the beard has fallen like a cloud into my lap. He hesitates, though, at the mustache. He would so like to keep such an impressive badge of manhood, this mustache that curls over my upper lip and swings gallantly off on each side. He points and looks at me with hopeful eyes, and when I say, "All off," and wave my hand, his brow sinks in resignation. "Clean?" he says, less a question than a sulking fact. "Clean shave!" I answer. He has, however, left sideburns and now his small scissors chirp like a tiny bird, shaping and grooming them to respectability. I don't really want them but I know when to give ground, and I cede this minor territory of my face to him.

Now the true shave can commence, and the gears that have probably swung countless patrons down for fifty years, if not a century, abruptly drop me back. First there is the spray of some refreshing fragrant water and the delicate ministrations of fingertips that softly but firmly work the potion into the skin, tracing and retracing the same ridges and slopes, the divots and crests of cheek and chin for minutes on end. Then, like a master presiding over his tea ceremony, he handles the stainless steel cup, lays the black-whiskered brush on top across its edge, and applies the thick gold paste of the cream in a precise dollop across the brush's flank.

I watch all of this in the mirror through dreamily sleepy lids three-quarters closed as if I were meditating, and join him as spectator in the moment-to-moment calm of ritual. The soft black bristles sweep and circle across my face, working up a rich lather, and like the fragrant water, the brush too at its master's instigation moves over and over and over my face, less a simple utilitarian act and more another massage, a caress, a swirling message of caring from one human to another, from one man to another. The shave he will give me will be so thorough, so close, that I could never achieve it on my own. For how many millennia has one man drawn a sharp blade across another man's neck in a quiet corner, like one monkey grooming another in the calm of a tree limb, the concentration breeding silence, the silence breeding trust, the trust breeding friendship? We are two men from opposite ends of the earth, but nevertheless two men, and we share this moment.

At the insistence of the brush my eyes close fully and I lose myself in my thoughts, which drift to the sweetness of men's bodies touching and colliding in all sorts of ways here in my travels. Two twentysomethings walk down the street in Delhi holding hands or curling one pinky with another or with a hand on a shoulder and a forearm resting on a back. High school boys on the bus in Dehradun joke with each other, an arm collaring a neck, hand against a chest or a belly. In the far north at the guest-house in Mussoorie, the very handsome and charming manager, Sunil, tells me the pages I have just printed out on the hotel's computer are at no charge and puts his arm around my waist and gives me a small squeeze and a smile.

My partner and I have traveled together here and have both been confused, charmed, and tormented by these alien gestures of intimacy. Is it all merely the consequence of so many, many bodies crushed together in this place where personal space is nil on buses, trains, or on the street where people, rickshaws, cars, cows, and donkeys jostle in fraught movement? Is it innocent touch or do pinkies not only curl into each other but also into belt loops, pulling bulging crotch to bulging crotch and wet tongue to wet tongue? And cannot this also be in its own way innocent? Why shouldn't men's friendship extend to and encompass the mutual quenching of physical needs before marriage, or instead of it? Perhaps it's a fantasy to imagine that here the borders of sexuality might draw themselves differently, the only treason being to never move beyond this to marriage and children. (I think of my own mother far away in space and time in Rhode Island in 1992 wailing when she found out: "I will never have grandchildren!")

It's minutes into the languorous swabbing across my face that I realize the barber's crotch is pressed against my shoulder as he works, apparently in unconscious need to better angle in for a good lather. Were he one of the men with thin arms bulging in sinewy muscles and shining white smiles, my body would boil over in fever (and will in just a few days in a masseur's hut on the banks of a backwater canal) but this old man is almost womanly in his kindness, neutered in my mind by the years between us and by the ritual relation of this intimate transaction. Because we are two humans who relentlessly sprout hair on our faces that requires careful removal, these bodies and their tending engender caring. Perhaps this is what it means to be human, this shedding of our animal evidence together. Because we are two men who know without words just how to open up the neck for the best sweep of the blade and bring this ritual into being together, these bodies and their tending engender gender in this sexed conference against animality. Perhaps this is what it means to be a man, this mingling in sameness, this homosocial comradery.

My barber, whose name I never learn, opens up a cabinet to retrieve a fresh razor blade and slips it into the straightedge. As he does this, my partner steps into the Shalimar Saloon, back from his walk around the block. What does Barber think of us? How does he read the text of us? My partner steps into the back waiting room to watch TV, and the shave truly commences. Barber tenderly cups my forehead and shifts me this way and that, pinches my nose, pushes a cheek one way and then the other. His strokes are short and careful with intermittent swipes on squares of paper. This blade could knit us together as fellow men or cleave us apart in a bright-red ribbon. If he knew I fantasized about the men falling against each other in the streets, about the charming smile of the manager at my hotel, which way would the razor swipe? Could he know this about me and about the man I love waiting in the back room and could the fraternity of caring still hold?

After the shave with just a few accidental drops of blood, he pats me down with bracing alcohol and each time I think we've finished with each other, he pulls out one and then another cream and calmly massages every part of my face over and over. Fingertip-taps, full-palmed mangles, interlinked finger-jiggles with first one lotion, then another, then another in a prescribed ritual, and I relax again.

Eventually it is over, imperceptibly, like a cloud lifting off a mountain. The chair is eased up, the drape removed, Barber scrutinizes his work with a patient eye, and I wonder if I had even had a father growing up would he have loved me the way this man loves me right now.

Field

Marco

Succession

That

Because of this   wound

the two of us alone

Her

obsession with forgetting his name

fingered,   over and over again,

left me

test

touch

Where there were

Any   one but   me

response when questioned

was a mania

whose edges never heal

Christ,   you went under

for how long

(Are you really here?)   (No, you're not.)

root   down for hidden memory

I am the end, succeeding

His absence hung above   everything refracting

                    uncles, real and   constructed

would have guessed   the plot twist   long ago

                 when I was four was a terror

           ruling like a   misplaced star over my house

how could she   ask me to father   into this world the next?

                    son-smitten   husband-hungry

              and harrowed so   the buried might rise

              and back up   more easily

                 again empty-handed

every   thing

    lacunae into every solid shape   until

    but I made sure, must have,   not to know

I also erased forcibly, repeatedly, a mania.   Her need for

That

Because of this   father who never was

widow-weary

and now?

barely any

who knew

what was

a secret

a secret

I too am

a secret

a secret

a secret

a secret

a secret

a secret

edge   was discernible.   His

                          only that I was   not theirs

                                          so obvious

          bent   light around its darkness

    could   unfather me   makes me

              a father   who never was

should   be

                      shuttled round

              un-overheard

                      well-pretended

          woven tight

                      black seed

with

    presence addressed   just minutes away,

       required effort.

  warped floorboards   shut doors

  wonder whether   speaking will

  unstringing the net that ties me to the future

    only a black beak shove, delight in the violence of

    only cotyledon caught eidolon caw tattle on

   only the patient curl and drill of root

  only scarring lets water in

planted deep

dark moon   whose other face is all light shining

Where   there were   aunts

where earthquakes simmered.

unmother me.

refusing

only the bloodied fingers of the buried furiously scratching

looking for what

lacks

cracks

nothing

                on some other sky.

    who whispered,

Any man might be   enough

                        Her grief

        That   I have felt

(because of this)   to the light   any surface,

transitiveness; remains after everything else

openness; remains after every peel

(Are you?)   parent material

"You're just like him,"   when   no one was   listening

to make me   man enough

when she   learned I was gay: "I will never have grandchildren."

like an orphan

flowers into seed

is a shame I carry   and will not let go.

but even singularities gleam dark   against the brighter night.

to be alive

Because of this wound fingered, over and over again, whose edges never heal, how could she ask me to father into this world the next? Because of this father who never was I too am a father who never was, unstringing the net that ties me to the future, refusing (because of this) to the light any surface, but even singularities gleam dark against the brighter night.

That obsession with forgetting his name was a mania ruling like a misplaced star over my house. That a secret could unfather me makes me wonder whether speaking will unmother me. That I have felt like an orphan is a shame I carry and will not let go.

the two of us alone left me son-smitten husband-hungry widow-weary a secret should be only the bloodied fingers of the buried furiously scratching

Her response when questioned once when I was four was a terror I also erased forcibly, repeatedly, a mania. Her need for a secret bent light around its darkness, warped floorboards, shut doors where earthquakes simmered. Her grief when she learned I was gay: "I will never have grandchildren."

test Christ, you went under and harrowed so the buried might rise a secret shuttled round only a black beak shove, delight in the violence of looking for what to be alive

Anyone but me would have guessed the plot twist long ago but I made sure, must have, not to know, what was so obvious required effort. Any man might be enough to make me man enough.

touch for how long and now? a secret un-overheard only cotyledon caught eidolon caw tattle on lacks transitiveness; remains after everything else

Where there were uncles, real and constructed, who knew only that I was not theirs. Where there were aunts who whispered, "You're just like him," when no one was listening.

(Are you really here?) (No, you're not.) a secret well-pretended only the patient curl and drill of root cracks openness; remains after every peel flowers into seed

His absence hung above everything refracting lacunae into every solid shape until barely any edge was discernible. His presence addressed just minutes away, dark moon whose other face is all light shining on some other sky.

root down for hidden memory, and back up more easily a secret woven tight only scarring lets water in

I am the end, succeeding everything with nothing.

again empty handed a secret black seed planted deep (Are you?)

parent material

We'd

we'd, you [and you] and I, conditionally

share a common history

      acknowledge that   we created   each other

          force   the world to reckon   with us

talk   about philosophy   and what it could   do for us

                       admire   flowers together

ornament   our shared   life

          obligate   others to make way

cancel all   our debts

      make sure the doors were shut at night and open all day long unroll   yarn and knit ourselves into   wings

anticipate   each other's follies

curate   museums memorializing   our deeds

measure   the world   against   our steps

build   factories firing   our names into the sky

code   our DNA into the weave of   our oh-so-dapper jackets

acclimate to the turbulence of   hourly merging   systems

correlate the night sky's brightness with the depth of our shared joy

gratefully thank   the stability of three-   legged stools

look from one   to the other, one   to the other, day   after day

ascertain   our longitude by   the meeting of our shadows

nurse   every   stray, never us   who are always home

roam the countryside   pulling every bird from kin's cross

drink maté in   the afternoon in a ritual   all our own

cross the need   for compensatory   fetishes off our lists

invite all the families   from all the directions   to our table

Coffee House Press began as a small letterpress operation in 1972 and has grown into an internationally renowned nonprofit publisher of literary fiction, essay, poetry, and other work that doesn't fit neatly into genre categories.

Coffee House is both a publisher and an arts organization. Through our *Books in Action* program and publications, we've become interdisciplinary collaborators and incubators for new work and audience experiences. Our vision for the future is one where a publisher is a catalyst and connector.

LITERATURE
is not the same thing as
PUBLISHING

Funder Acknowledgments

Coffee House Press is an internationally renowned independent book publisher and arts nonprofit based in Minneapolis, MN; through its literary publications and *Books in Action* program, Coffee House acts as a catalyst and connector—between authors and readers, ideas and resources, creativity and community, inspiration and action.

Coffee House Press books are made possible through the generous support of grants and donations from corporations, state and federal grant programs, family foundations, and the many individuals who believe in the transformational power of literature. This activity is made possible by the voters of Minnesota through a Minnesota State Arts Board Operating Support grant, thanks to the legislative appropriation from the Arts and Cultural Heritage Fund. Coffee House also receives major operating support from the Amazon Literary Partnership, Jerome Foundation, McKnight Foundation, Target Foundation, and the National Endowment for the Arts (NEA). To find out more about how NEA grants impact individuals and communities, visit www.arts.gov.

Coffee House Press receives additional support from Bookmobile; Dorsey & Whitney LLP; Fredrikson & Byron, P.A.; Kenneth Koch Literary Estate; the Matching Grant Program Fund of the Minneapolis Foundation; Mr. Pancks' Fund in memory of Graham Kimpton; the Schwab Charitable Fund; and the U.S. Bank Foundation.

The Publisher's Circle of Coffee House Press

Publisher's Circle members make significant contributions to Coffee House Press's annual giving campaign. Understanding that a strong financial base is necessary for the press to meet the challenges and opportunities that arise each year, this group plays a crucial part in the success of Coffee House's mission.

Recent Publisher's Circle members include many anonymous donors, Patricia A. Beithon, Anitra Budd, Andrew Brantingham, Dave & Kelli Cloutier, Mary Ebert & Paul Stembler, Jocelyn Hale & Glenn Miller, the Rehael Fund-Roger Hale/Nor Hall of the Minneapolis Foundation, Randy Hartten & Ron Lotz, Dylan Hicks & Nina Hale, William Hardacker, Kenneth & Susan Kahn, Stephen & Isabel Keating, the Kenneth Koch Literary Estate, Cinda Kornblum, Jennifer Kwon Dobbs & Stefan Liess, the Lambert Family Foundation, the Lenfestey Family Foundation, Sarah Lutman & Rob Rudolph, the Carol & Aaron Mack Charitable Fund of the Minneapolis Foundation, Gillian McCain, Malcolm S. McDermid & Katie Windle, Mary & Malcolm McDermid, Daniel N. Smith III & Maureen Millea Smith, Peter Nelson & Jennifer Swenson, Enrique & Jennifer Olivarez, Alan Polsky, Robin Preble, Jeffrey Sugerman & Sarah Schultz, Nan G. Swid, Grant Wood, and Margaret Wurtele.

For more information about the Publisher's Circle
and other ways to support Coffee House Press books, authors, and
activities, please visit www.coffeehousepress.org/pages/donate
or contact us at info@coffeehousepress.org.

Marco Wilkinson has been a horticulturist, a farmer, and an editor. He currently teaches creative writing at James Madison University and Antioch University's MFA program. He has been the recipient of an Ohio Arts Council Award for Individual Excellence and fellowships from the Hemera Foundation, Craigardan, and the Bread Loaf Environmental Writer's Conference. *Madder* is his first book.

Madder was designed by
Bookmobile Design & Digital Publisher Services.
Text is set in Garamond Premier Pro.

tally the treasure

have the luxury   to believe in something

    expect the ground   to ripen at our approach

transcribe   our footprints, dictate   our stumbles

              loose laughter   from its leash

occupy ourselves   more than survival, melancholy, invisibility

    feel the sun's warmth on our faces   just one of many loves

pass the black pebble   warm from one hand   to another

estimate the weight of lost time,   not ever knowing   firsthand

          plant a tree over each of our future graves

enjoy each other's company   without wondering at an empty chair

    remember (grandparents) and anticipate (grandchildren)

    be the gravity well   of our own   solar system

be happy

Coda

Fable: Cenicienta's Son
Tells a Story

"María rotos de sueño (María Landó)"

The truth is I don't even know if I am a worm or a child or a man or something past all of those, if there are wings on my back or just glancing reflections off the walls of my life. My memory plays tricks on me, and my vision has a habit of doubling, tripling, swimming with ghosts and shadows. Maybe I am the product of another lifetime. If I ask these mirrors what is fair and what is foul, will they answer?

"There was and there wasn't a time in my life before you were born," she would tell me the few times I asked as a young child. I learned early to stop asking, before I could articulate rational arguments against her irrational glare and puffs of air through nostrils set hard like stone. This learning sank like sand to the bottom of the ocean and sedimented into ground-truth. She turned and walked away, her wide bare feet falling like receding thunder after a lightning strike that never happened.

She never wore shoes of any kind—not boots or sandals or flats or heels or espadrilles or flip-flops—and so the soles of her feet grew leathery and black, her toes horned and bunioned. Though the other women in her close-knit circle of relatives and old-country acquaintances, all married and shod and respectable, alternately pitied and scorned her naked feet, she took no notice of them. Like the strategy of willful forgetting she employed in the face of her son's impertinent questions, she waltzed through the family parties and get-togethers, the copetines and the fiestas and the summer afternoon asados, as if she were one of them, daring with her cracked soles and the massive spread of her toes any one of those women to point out her difference. This habit she had of swinging in arcs through any space she crossed made it awkward to be near her, though everyone accommodated it, and so no one ever stood still but the whole room would shiver and sway itself around her.

All of this seemed at once completely normal and unsettlingly wrong. For me "there wasn't" a time before my birth and so what else could all this be but this world, simply the world? For all of them "there was" a whole world of time before me, and the black kernel of my being was passed in secret handshakes and pass-offs among them in a counterpoint to my mother's maniacal dancing.

"Ceni! Ceni!" one of my aunts blurted out late one night after too many drinks at a family party. "Ceni, I want you to know that if you ever have to go on welfare, that I am here for you. I will help you, O.K.?" And with that her "sister" managed to simultaneously offer her generosity with one hand and take away my mother's dignity and delusional pride with the other. She smiled across the table, foolish, drunk, self-satisfied with her catty cleverness. Everyone else tensed up, waiting for the response. My mother's face turned to stone for a moment, then relaxed as she hefted one foot on to the other leg's knee and began picking at her thick yellowed toenails right there at the table.

No one was known by their birth names. What does a birth name tell you about a person other than the stupid ill-founded aspirations of their parents? No, a proper nickname bestowed by one's circle captured the essence and the role of a person. It identified them: not only signified but imbued them with significance. And so "Ceni" was merely a nickname for a nickname, "Cenicienta," so long hers that no one even remembered her real name. What else could she be, this one who swept the ashes of every previous day out of the oven in the predawn darkness and set the fire she would tend there every day to feed her parents and her six other siblings? She was always covered in that ghastly whiteness, a shade among the living. Maybe that was how she managed to slip through borders and under the eyes of anyone who mattered.

I have no idea because while there was, there also wasn't. What is this double vision but fiction? As a child, before questions sprouted from my mouth, I would stir the ashes and look through them, illuminated by the cold sun, and try to make out that time before me. Every day it was different but it always slipped away. Now, I think I know more but still it is only ash thrown into the air, a shifting fiction.

There was and there wasn't a time before, when she was thirty years old and already tired, a dwindling fire drowning in its own ash, and she found herself in a bright land. Every day she assiduously scrubbed herself bright, washed her fiery red hair and ran a comb through its length, strapped her unruly feet into the latest fashions, her toes crushed into points and her heels raised up higher and higher, a small gesture toward the rising tide of hope she had in her own life. She whispered her real name to herself each morning in the steamed-up mirror of her daily cleansing.

"Who is the fairest of them all?" the mirror demanded.

"----," she would answer.

But in a bright land, if it is to be bright, shadows must be swept, mopped, polished, hefted, folded away. A newcomer like her was there to keep things bright. Each night she returned to her tidy apartment, covered again. It was as if the ashes poured out of each pore in little tumbling falls. "Cenicienta."

The only thing that burned hotter than her hope for new life in this bright land was her shame at the daily accrual of ash on her body. What to do with all of it? She collected it in a small box, scrubbed it out of the shower stall, and threw those gray-black scales into the white powder, too, ran the comb through her tresses and used a toothpick to strip her teeth of the gray mortar between. The box safely hidden under her bed, she lay down exhausted and dreamed of another, whispering her own name, "----," into the fire of her hair.

Every day was the same: the rising up, the furious scrubbing and cleaning away of the night's desire-laden ash, the circuit from shining house to shining house to run away other people's shadows, the late-night return to the tiny apartment, the hour-long scrubbing and cleaning away of a day's accumulation of ash into a small box. Funny how the box never filled, always ready to take in more and more over the years.

And then one morning when she slipped the lid off carefully, lest some betraying cinders might spill, she found instead a pair of diamond high-heeled pumps, gleaming in their hardness. What was this? Then she noticed that motes of ash no longer fell from her tumbling hair or sifted in little plumes from her fingertips.

She raced to the mirror and demanded of it this time, "Who is the fairest of them all?"

It answered with her reflection, submissive.

For the first time ever, she took the day off from her appointed rounds. Let someone else tend to shadows. These shoes were bright and would make her bright as well in this bright land. Let her invisibility shift, from shadow to shimmer. She carefully lifted them out of the box. They were light, like the solidification of sunlight pouring through pure air. She slipped them on easily, her once-wild feet tamed over the years by so many other shoes now woefully inadequate in the light of this shining pair.

She took a step.

Glittering pain shot up her leg, a fire in her head. Dizzy, she looked down to see blood flowing freely and refracting through the prismatic glimmer of the shoes. Breathing in and steeling herself, she took another step. Scarlet blossoms of agony erupted. No! This was hers. This was not torture but a miracle. She would make it so.

Out in the light of the streets of the bright land, she walked in practiced, short steps and was surprised to be seen by the inhabitants who had never noticed her before. Women smiled, men paused. One in particular paused, stopped as if he remembered hearing his name a long time ago, and only now the echo of it flooded his brain like diamond light. He grabbed her and threw her into arcs of motion, the sky spinning like a prism, colors shining everywhere. This was everything, this was staring at the sun.

Even amid the waltzing arcs of pleasure, she hatched a plan. If ashes and dreams could coalesce into diamond-hard light, then what could her ferocious will to shine make of diamonds and blood and the tight turns of this man in this bright land? Compacting, compounding, smelting against the anvil of her indignity at so many years of shadow-work, diamonds were ground down, blood thickened and bubbled, light laced itself through in nets.

When she was done, she held in her sweaty self-satisfied arms a little glimmering worm of a life, whose faceless mouth twitched in all directions until she nudged it to her breast. She looked down to find that the diamond shoes were gone, eaten up no doubt by her alchemical work and leaving only bloodied feet, and then looked up to see the counterpoint of her swinging dance let go, horrified by the suckling monster, too-solid product of himself. Does retreating light, like air, breeze past one's cheek?

Immediately she was in darkness, returned to shadows. She stuffed her glowing grub inside herself, a shadow inside the shadow of her shadow, and ran barefoot home. From then on she returned to sweeping shadows and ashes up for the brighter folk, and though she continued to brush the ashes off her own skin, it was a half-hearted gesture culminating in a dismissive sweep of a broom over the front door's threshold. Let the wind take the ash away, or not. She no longer cared. Under her skin and under the ash, a dim light glowed, her one and only possession. Two things were banned from her life from that moment on: mirrors and shoes. If she needed to see herself, she preferred to look in the gloom of musty closets or the murk at the bottom of cellar stairs over the pure cruelty of reflected light. And shoes, what need did she have of them? They slowed her down in her work, she concluded, and she had no time for the ridiculousness of her sisters' petty fashions.

But then the glowing grub grew small teeth and pinprick eyes. It gnawed its way through skin and ash, out of her web of grief and into the world. A slick mewling thing, all mouth, all questions. Now it was no longer the mirror demanding answers from her, but instead this relentlessly growing brightness in her shrine of shadows and cinders.

Her apartment had a little utility closet and so, furious at her child's insistence on being born out of her body and out of her life, she fitted the closet with a seamless set of mirrors—floor, ceiling, four walls—and a candle, and locked him in. Let him eat light, she thought.

And so I have, all these years. Now it is the walls that demand answers, but all I have is myself. I speak and my speech is wings buffeting the silvered glass. I dance in arcs and don't even know if I have feet. I look out and I see skin but not my own. I look in and I see a light, these wings aflame, and a plume of ash, swirling.

[Echo: The Sound of My Father]

"There's no place he doesn't look
And looking he loses himself"

Just a few years ago I learned from my cousin Elsa that she had heard my never-known father's voice when she was a child. She mentioned it casually, never registering the devastation that swept across my face. "Oh sure, he used to come by and visit my parents all the time."

It lives on: some faintest echo still travels through the expanse of her life. Its timbre and cadence, its gravelly bass notes or its clear glass-like pitch or its trills of immigrant *r*'s rendering homely English into something warmer and stranger—it rolls across her memory even if hidden and forgotten. Did he learn English before he ever left Uruguay, and so at the foot of some teacher tamed his open-mouthed Ríoplatense Spanish into more careful curves of vowels and pursed-lip consonants? Or like my mother, did he learn on the fly from Sunday comics and soap operas? Was his laughter full-throated or merely a chuckle? Did he command a room with a boom or retreat into the background in whispers?

> (Notice my slip into the past tense.
> My absent invisible soundless father
> who is always only a thing of the past

Show me your face before your father spoke.

> because not knowing
> if he is even alive or dead
> it seems safest
> to consign him to death. Irretrievable,
> I make him irretrievable.)

And if I asked Elsa what he sounded like, she probably wouldn't be able to tell me. How many sounds of chance encounters litter our lives and we take no notice of what, for another, might sound like the birth of the universe? How poor I am, to need to beg someone else to dredge from the scrap heap of their history some rotting thread of memory. How proud I am, that I will never ask her to tell me, to slip from her mouth the already-chewed and softened, the half-forgotten memory of an echo, and feed me with it.

> Old crooked pine tree,
> Summer swallows rise in flight:
> Who could look away?

That's what I wrote to him when I was twenty-one, heard his name uttered in my ear for the first time from a mother infuriated that she would be made to speak it, and found his address in the phone book. Marco _____. It was always there, one line among many. Pristine, never smudged off the cheap, pulpy white pages; never touched before. It turned out he lived in the same small town that I grew up in, just a few minutes away. Had I heard him ask for a book of stamps while waiting in the post office? Did his smile and small talk with the checkout girl at the market carry two aisles over to me?

And what's more, every relative's home that hosted me had also opened its doors to him, even after he walked out on my mother and me. At parties and cookouts and on casual unimportant afternoons after work, on days when my mother and I were elsewhere, he would pass through their front doors and sit down in their kitchens or their living rooms for a whiskey or a maté. He was friends with all of them. Every substitute mother, every distant uncle, every cousin like a sibling in my life saw his face and heard his voice. Was that the smell of his cigarettes or cologne that lingered in the air by Tí'Bibí's kerosene stove or on the soft peach walls of Ina's house? Was that subtle earthquake running through my childhood the echo of his voice?

I drove by the tidy little ranch house listed in the phone book, I wrote my enigmatic poem about pines and swallows and dropped it in the mail, but I never dialed those digits and held the receiver to my ear. Though his old and broken voice might have spun through the copper wires, I am sure nothing would have or could have emerged in my world. Only empty wind, black and obliterating, like the voice of God from a cleft in the mountain, or from a burning bush that, once lit, sets the whole world on fire. Though the small note fell into the open mouth of the mailbox, no answer ever echoed back. Across the barrier of two worlds nothing ever passes.

And then the listing disappeared from subsequent editions of the phonebook. Even silence fled, and there was only one world in this world.

Botanical Notes

p. 67 *xylem:* the vascular cells of a plant that conduct water up from its roots to its leaves. Their counterpart, phloem, transports sugars from leaves down to roots. What is interesting about xylem cells is that they only become useful in death. They grow in order to construct the rigid cell walls around them. As they die off, the walls on either end of a xylem cell decay away along with the cell's interior, leaving a row of these empty husks end to end for water to flow through. Water is pulled up these long tubes for anywhere from a few inches to hundreds of feet by the physics of capillary action and the exhalations of water vapor by leaves high up in the sun.

p. 71 *One can feed small birds in their cages shreds of madder . . . :* Maude Grieve, in her entry on madder in *A Modern Herbal,* describes this effect of staining animal bones, especially those "nearest to the heart."

p. 75 *Miles out from anywhere . . . :* Donald Culross Peattie reports in *A Natural History of Trees of Eastern and Central North America* that the pine forests of the eastern seaboard were once so vast that when they released their yellow pollen, great clouds of it would be carried far out to sea and sometimes envelop ships on the Atlantic.

p. 97 *Deep in the green, clasped tight in a downward-mouthing cup of matter . . . :* When flowers are pollinated a complex process begins with pollen sending a tube burrowing down the flower's style to its ovary. Two sperm cells travel down this tube and through the micropyle into the ovule, which is like a cup. Inside, one sperm cell joins with the egg cell and the other merges with what are called the two polar nuclei. These three will form the food source for the zygote created by sperm and egg, eventually being used up entirely.

p. 102 *pinnatifid:* the shape of leaves that are pinnate-like. Pinnate leaves are compound leaves comprised of several individual leaflets. They are "pinnate," or feather-like, in that the arrangement of leaflets along a central axis is like the arrangement of individual barbs that together form a bird's feather. Pinnatifid leaves do not have individual leaflets but are so sharply toothed along their margins that they seem to be pinnate.

p. 107 *crucifer:* the plant family that includes shepherd's purse (as well as cabbage, mustard, and others). Plants in this family have four flower petals radiating out in a cross shape.

p. 107 *raceme:* one of the kinds of inflorescences or groupings of individual flowers on a plant. Racemes, corymbs, umbels, cymes, thyrses, panicles, and glomerules are all different arrangements of groups of flowers on plants.

p. 117 *totipotent:* "all-powerful." Plants described as totipotent have the ability to regenerate themselves entirely from a single cell.

p. 126 *humus:* the smallest remnant of plant matter after the decomposition process. Humus acts as a sponge in soil for attracting and holding nutrients. Incredibly stable, it may remain for thousands of years without further transformation. Humus is the past nourishing the present.

p. 143 *succession:* the way life inexorably moves from bare rock to lichens and mosses to plants and eventually to mature grasslands or forests. Each form gives way to and is subsumed by and forms the matrix for what follows it. What are the inevitable products of our lives? What are the measures of a life's success? Is what succeeds us our success?

Acknowledgments

Earlier versions of the following have appeared, sometimes in shortened or altered forms, in the following journals:

"Root: Burdock," *Kenyon Review Online.*

"This Plain-Sight Treasure: Some Rules for Foraging in Waste Spaces," *Taproot.*

"Flower: Madder" and "Substitutions 1: A House of Swinging Doors: This Future Life *(Calvatia gigantea),*" *DIAGRAM.*

"Seed: Shepherd's Purse," *Kenyon Review.*

"Substitutions 2: Among Men," *AWAY.*

"Succession," *Seneca Review.*

Thank you to Oberlin College Press for permission to reprint "Hide and Seek," by Vasko Popa.

Thanks also to Susana Baca for permission to reprint "María Landó," by César Calvo, as sung to her by the poet himself. Your luminous rendition of this song is the origin point of this book.

Thank you to the staff of Coffee House Press, especially Erika Stevens, Carla Valadez, and Kellie M. Hultgren, for giving life to this book.

Thank you to the Stonecoast MFA community, where the seeds of this book were sown, especially to my faculty mentors Cait Johnson, Debra Marquart, and Barbara Hurd.

Thank you to Crosshatch Center for Art and Ecology and Craigardan for writing residencies and the gifts of solitude, camaraderie, and the natural world.

Thank you to the Village Zendo sangha and especially Roshi Enkyo O'Hara for nurturing this dragon. Thank you to the Empty Field sangha for being good spiritual friends. Deep bows.

Thank you to my gardening teachers Caroline Burgess and Peter Nelson for this love of the green world.

Thank you to Gregory Allen, Janet Fiskio, Judy Seicho Fleischman, Mushim Patricia Ikeda, Greggor Mattson, Laurie McMillin, Julie Patton, DJ Savarese, Emily Savarese, Ralph Savarese, Nancy Seaton, Sun Yung Shin, Brian Teare, Ted Toadvine, David Walker, Nicole Walker, and David Young for your encouragement and support over the years.

Thank you to family who answered when asked.

Finally, thank you to Kazim Ali, who has always believed there was a story to tell and without whom this weed would have perished long ago.